Be Your Own Miracle

Empowering Pathways to Unleash Your Inner Resilience

Be Your Own Miracle

Published by Motion Media International
Editors: Kit Brookman and Eric Wyman
Cover Design: Motion Media International
Typesetting & Assembly: Motion Media International
Printing: Amazon and Ingram Sparks

Creator: John Spender - Annette Forsythe - Primary Authors
Title: *Be Your Own Miracle - Empowering Pathways to Unleash Your Inner Resilience*
ISBN Digital: 978-1-925919-66-0
ISBN Print: 978-1-925919-67-7
Subjects: Motivation and Inspiration, Spirituality

TABLE OF CONTENTS

PREFACE

I n a world often filled with challenges, uncertainties, and self-doubt, it is easy to lose sight of the extraordinary potential that lies within each of us. We often find ourselves waiting for miracles to happen, believing that they are reserved for the chosen few or bestowed upon us by some external force. But what if we told you that you have the power to be your own miracle?

In this book, we delve into our journey's, armed with the belief that miracles are not just external events but are within our reach, waiting to be unleashed. We have experienced firsthand the transformative power of tapping into our inner strength, resilience, and unwavering belief in ourselves.

Being Your Own Miracle is a heartfelt exploration of our personal stories, as well as a guide to help you unlock the miracles that reside within you. Through our shared wisdom, experiences, and practical insights, we invite you to embark on a transformative journey of self-discovery and empowerment. Drawing upon our triumphs and tribulations, we endeavor to take you on a voyage of understanding, encouraging you to embrace your uniqueness, ignite your passions, and conquer your fears. We hope to inspire you to redefine what it means to be a miracle, shifting the focus from external forces to the incredible potential that lies dormant within your own being.

This book is not a quick fix or a magic potion. It is a roadmap—a collection of principles, practices, and reflections that will guide you towards realizing your full potential. It invites you to embrace your flaws, celebrate your strengths, and harness the power of self-belief to create miracles in your own life. We are all miracles in mind, body and spirit. Somehow during the aging process, we forget that we have everything we need inside of us.

As you embark on this journey, remember that you are not alone. We are here to walk beside you, offering our support, wisdom, and encouragement every step of the way. We hope our stories will touch your heart, challenge your perceptions, and inspire you to take courageous actions that will bring forth the miracles you deserve.

So, if you are ready to awaken the miracle within you, to break free from self-imposed limitations, and to create a life that surpasses your wildest dreams, then open the pages of this book. Allow us to be your guides, mentors, and companions on the extraordinary adventure of being your own miracle.

May this book be a catalyst for transformative change, empowering you to embrace your innate potential, and reminding you that you possess the power to be your own miracle.

With love, light, and boundless possibilities,

John Spender & Annette Forsythe

"Miracles start to happen when you give as much energy to your dreams as you do to your fears."

~ Richard Wilkins

CHAPTER ONE

Courage

By Annette Forsythe

D o you see yourself as others see you? Or do you see yourself as you think others see you? You would be surprised to know other people usually "see" you more clearly than you see yourself. I have spent a good deal of my life trying to blend into the background and not be noticed. I lacked confidence in myself and doubted my worth, defining my value by my overweight appearance. I was my own worst critic, and it seemed obvious to me that everyone else shared my own harsh judgments of myself.

In reality, if you were to meet me on the street, you would meet a seemingly confident woman who is an accomplished businessperson and a Chief Financial Officer for 22 years, someone who has been married for 41 years and raised four incredible women. Best of all, now I am Nonni to three precious grandchildren and a grand pup. Wow! This lady has her act together, you would think. But I will let you in on a secret. Looks are deceiving. Behind my confident exterior is not what you would think, not even close.

When my daughters were young, I realized if I wanted to have a say about things that involved them, I would have to earn the right. Put up or shut up. So, a volunteer was born, and oh my goodness, the amazing opportunities! The intention had started as a way of being involved in my own children's lives, but it grew into an aim to make a difference for all the children in our community.

I started small. I became a Homeroom Mom. Small children just love you; they do not judge. I enjoyed making treats and doing crafts. What mom does not enjoy a field trip? Full disclosure—I also loved any opportunity that allowed me to see my girls in action. This was working. So began my connection to the Parent Teacher Association (PTA).

I had no idea what I had just gotten myself into. Different committees followed, then committee chair positions. By this time, the girls were getting involved in sports. Did we not need to have a presence there as well? So, my husband would coach, and I sat on the various youth sports boards. (Sports could take up a chapter of their own—back to the PTA.)

My time on the nominating committee was the catalyst that landed me on the Executive Board. I worked my way up the ladder, and in the blink of an eye, I was President of the Hackettstown Elementary PTA for two years. Then the Hackettstown Foundation for Educational Excellence (HFEE) came into existence, and it was not long before I was the Executive Director. Between the two positions, I made quite the name for myself, doing what was important to me. I made a difference for my daughters and every other student in our town. I felt blessed.

The opportunities were incredible. There was public speaking in front of school administrators and parents. There was raising and distributing grant funding for the teachers. I presented a program at the New Jersey Board of Education Convention, and I got to work with the Geraldine Dodge Foundation through the same program. But what no one realized is that, in taking up these great opportunities, I was forcing myself every step of the way. I was still the same woman who wanted to blend into the background and not be noticed. But I made myself do it. I closed my eyes and jumped. I jumped into this world, where I began to learn about my limits. I guess my lack of limits would be more accurate.

How does someone who is painfully shy take on a public persona? It was not easy. But my motivation to make a better life for my girls trumped my fear of putting myself in a position to be judged. I lacked courage, at least I thought I did, but by forcing myself to take one step after another, I was learning how to tap into it. True, I was not preparing for battle or trying to save the world. No lives were being saved. No one was in danger. But is being brave in extreme situations really all there is to courage?

Merriam-Webster defines courage as "the mental or moral strength to venture, persevere and withstand danger, fear or difficulty." It is one's ability to process fear in a dangerous situation. Diving deeper, courage drives our actions. It can come in a gesture or a step into uncertain territory. Courage is our ability to do things that frighten us, take the unpopular approach, and do the right thing. What frightens each of us might be different, but we can all tap into this inner power.

We know courage when we see it. Historically, there are so many people before us known for their courage. Harriet Tubman, Anne Frank, Rosa Parks, Mother Theresa, Martin Luther King, John and Robert Kennedy, just to name a few. However, there is a common thread that connects all these people. They all tapped into their inner powers to make a difference. And each of us has this same power within us. My friends, that kind of courage is there in you right now! All you must do is believe in yourself and acknowledge the energy you carry in you. Like anyone who has faced down their fears, it takes courage to believe in yourself, to recognize the power we hold inside us. And here is another secret: in the moments when you don't feel courage inside, you can borrow it.

Who do you know that exhibits the courage you wish you had? How do they behave and move through the world? What are their key traits? Borrow them until you can find your own. That is how I learned to take my first step. I held my breath, my knees were shaking, and I took a leap of faith when I jumped into my volunteer world.

Before every Back-to-School night, there would be a welcome speech by the PTA. My stomach would be in knots, and I would begin to sweat profusely before I stood up to speak. By the time I took the podium, I looked like a wet rat. Those were fight-or-flight moments. I am so grateful I chose to stay and fight, because these were the moments that prepared me for my growth journey.

I did not realize it at the time; it was only looking back that brought what I was doing to light. In those moments, I borrowed the courage of some incredible women who came before me. I learned lessons and took them to heart. These were the lessons that shaped my outlook and my ability to face my fears. It was always there. I just had to find it.

I am blessed to have had strong female role models. I do not consider myself a feminist, and I do appreciate how the female role has expanded through the years. We are strong-willed, free-speaking, educated, dynamic souls. We have learned to have it all. My lessons in courage were passed on to me by women I admire, love, and respect. Women who broke the mold. What an honor to pass these lessons on to my daughters.

Angelina Lioi Spendio

Angelina traveled to the United States from Bari, Italy, at 17 years of age. She was my maternal grandmother.

She was newly wed in an arranged marriage and three months pregnant when she followed her husband to a foreign country to make a new life. She never ceased to marvel at the sight of the Atlantic Ocean, the body of water that carried her across the world to a new life. Now that kind of journey into the unknown takes courage.

What did I know at 17? I was a silly teenager with a part-time job, worried if my friends would call and include me in their plans. I most certainly was not navigating life in a new world with a foreign language and a baby on the way. I cannot in my wildest dreams imagine the strength and courage it took to face down all the uncertainty involved in the idea of a better life for her and her growing family.

Behind her meek, young exterior, there was a woman that would forge ahead. Her place may have been home caring for my grandfather and raising her children, yet there was a determination that dripped with love while she created their "American Dream."

Extended family members followed, and they all settled within a few blocks of each other. There they stayed as they raised their families and followed the old country traditions. They did not drive; they walked everywhere. Nothing went to waste; they grew magnificent gardens with grape arbors. Their basement iceboxes were lined with jars of canned and pickled bounty.

There were rules and discipline, and boundaries were not crossed. There was respect. Roles were clearly defined, and there were strong work ethics. My grandfather was the patriarch, and my grandmother was the dutiful wife who kept the home and raised the family. The children were seen and not heard and had their specific roles in the family. It may have been an old-world existence, but my grandma was years ahead of her time. She was so smart—life smart, sometimes the most critical kind.

Grandma was the one who supported me when my husband and I were transferred out of state. She was the one who encouraged me when I nursed my babies. Her words of wisdom still guide me in my daily life. My favorite of her simple and profound sayings was, "You never know when something is right, but you always know if it's wrong." Or, "Listen to your heart, be honest. The truth is there." Were these the thoughts that were in her head when she embarked on her voyage to America?

When it was time for my husband and me to move, she counseled that when you love someone, you follow them to the ends of the Earth. These words surely came from her experience. She traveled across an ocean.

My grandmother was so proud that she was as old as the century. She was born in 1900 and lived to see the world change, and she changed and grew right along with it.

Grandma taught me to trust my heart. She gave me the courage to leap and adapt. I was blessed to be part of her 86 years of life.

Josephine Spendio Santangelo

Aunt Jo was my mom's younger sister. Aunt Jo was a newlywed when she decided she wanted a business. So she and her husband, Uncle John, traveled to New York City to meet the sales teams of the many bridal design houses. Josephine loved brides—a bridal shop would be the perfect business. The typical response from the sales teams they met was that they were not ready yet and should return home, but Josephine was not giving up. She and Uncle John returned home, but they were not discouraged. Tattler's Lane Bridal Shop was born shortly after that trip to New York. Aunt Jo did not even know how to sew, but she knew what she was passionate about and was willing to learn and work hard. By the time she retired at the young age of 90, in her 67-year career, she served 4 generations of brides in some families. She had the #1 bridal shop in Niagara Falls, earning countless awards for her dedication, commitment, and demanding work. In her career, Aunt Jo served over 22,000 brides, over 117,000 bridesmaids, as well as creating numerous mother of the bride dresses, prom dresses, and communion dresses.

I spent every summer of my childhood in that shop. I loved hanging out in the basement with all the ladies that worked there. I spent countless hours watching my aunt practicing her skills and found any excuse to be there, whether I was sewing clothes for my Barbie dolls, cleaning the showcases, vacuuming, or changing the window display so that I could be near the brides. Every woman that walked into the shop got the same treatment, whether they spent $100 or $10,000. Every bride was treated like a queen, like they were the most beautiful bride in the world. And Aunt Jo believed that they were, because that is what she saw, and so did I. Josephine was at the church to send every bride down the aisle so that their families could take in that unique beauty as well.

Everyone in town knew Josephine and loved her. Walking down Pine Avenue with her, we were stopped every ten feet by someone saying hello. I knew then that I wanted to live somewhere where everyone knew me too.

Aunt Jo always kept sight of the importance of giving back. She made sure that girls in need had prom dresses or communion dresses. Families in need were comforted knowing their beloved mothers, daughters, or sisters were laid to rest in a beautiful gown. These were heartfelt kindnesses that the recipients would never forget.

When we celebrated her retirement, over 100 Tattler's brides were there. The collection of wedding portraits was incredible to see, with each gown more outstanding than the next. Aunt Jo had a knack for foreseeing exactly how you should look.

I will always remain in awe of the many lives she has touched. But, of course, everyone knows and loves Josephine. Just mention her name in Niagara Falls and a story of her kindness will follow. And yet, it would have been so easy for her not to pursue her dream after the discouraging feedback from that early trip to New York City. Aunt Jo's courage lay in trusting that if she followed her passion, everything else (with a lot of hard work) would fall into place.

Aunt Jo fostered my desire to own a business. She taught me to take risks and believe in success when motivated by the right intentions.

I did relocate to a small town with my husband and growing family. I became an active volunteer in sports and education, and my name was well known in my community. I have owned a business for 22 years. There is just one significant difference. Let me admit right now, I will retire before the age of 90.

Josephine Serianni Granite

Not to be confused with Aunt Jo, Josephine was my Auntie Jo, and I was her Baby. It would not be an exaggeration to say I spent more nights a week with Auntie Jo and Uncle Jimmy than I did at my own house as a child.

If there ever was a real-life Auntie Mame, she was it. She lived every day with a zest for life and a spirit to live each day entirely like no one else I have ever met.

Auntie Jo taught me how to appreciate every moment. She taught me how to think of others and to add value to the world. She wanted me to be present and experience every magical moment life had to offer. From her example, I learned how to be grateful for God's blessings.

She would regularly come to pick me up from home and take me on an adventure. We would climb fences or brick walls and explore nature. Once, we climbed a brick wall in her backyard to reach a tree that housed a bird's nest and the cheeping hatchlings. We unexpectedly found another nest that day also. It was a red ant nest. That sent us running.

One afternoon, Auntie Jo raced to our house with carambola, a star fruit, so that I could experience the wonder of "its star-shaped slice." She taught me the importance of saving money, bringing it to the bank, and watching it grow. Auntie Jo taught me everything I know about being a lady and how to appreciate some of the finer things that life had to offer.

Auntie Jo had a few "principles" she never wavered from. I have lovingly called them "Josephine-isms."

1. You can tell the state of a woman's life by the form of her purse.
2. It is not going out to lunch if you cannot have a martini.
3. Always carry a bag of change because you never know when you might find a good card game.

The card games continue to elude me, but I save my change to this day, in a Louis Vuitton purse I paid for with the change I now keep inside it. Now, I save the change for my grandchildren. There were so many other Josephine-isms; these were her classics. To this day, when life feels out of control, the first thing I do is clean my purse.

Whenever I find myself in need of courage to embrace a new experience, I think of Auntie Jo, who never hesitated to climb a brick wall to reach a better view of the world, no matter how many ants' nests she might stir up along the way.

Mary Spendio Pascuzzi

Last on this list is my mother. Mom nurtured my heart. She was one of a kind. Mom loved with her entire being; anyone who walked into our home was welcomed with open arms. Those visitors were frequent as we lived in Florida and our whole extended family was in Niagara Falls, New York. It was always a happy time to be around our extended family.

I will not say that life was all roses. However, we had a perfectly normal relationship as mother and daughter. We fought, we laughed, we cried. I, of course, knew everything. I am quite sure I drove her to her wits' end at times—in fact, probably most of the time.

When she passed away too young, at 60, my world fell to pieces. I was seven months pregnant with my second child. When you have your mom, you have the world. No one else plays as many roles as possible in your life. Mom was my everything.

We had so many laughs at her expense. She was our "Little Woman," the glue that held our family together. Like her mother and sister, she was dynamic for her small stature and gifted in so many ways. When my dad became disabled and all their income had stopped, Mom could stretch a dollar further than anyone I have ever known. She was an incredible cook, and she made sure there was a hot meal on the table every night. Mom made so many sacrifices for my sister and me, even quitting her job when I was 13-years-old so that I would not come home to an empty house when my sister had left for college.

There is a mountain of stories I could tell about my mom. But the most important thing is simply this: no matter what was going on, I always knew that my mother loved me and that her love for me would never change. My mother's love gave me the strength and courage to do anything. I could lean on the power of that love to step into any kind of uncertainty, knowing her love would hold me up, even if I failed. If I have passed on anything to my girls, I pray this is the lesson they have adopted—that we can be a source of courage for others as well as for ourselves.

My mom gave me love, power, and courage. I miss her every day, and when I imagine what it would have been like to see her with my four girls, I picture her loving heart overflowing with joy and the girls feeling like the most loved people in the world. Love gives you the power to be courageous.

Marion Pascuzzi Gundling

Technically, my last role model came seven years before me, and yet she is my contemporary. My older sister Marion is the one who taught me all of my favorite (I mean bad) habits. We can still giggle like little schoolgirls and get into our fair share of trouble, especially when our father was still alive. Time just slips away when we are together. I was with Marion when I bought that Louis Vuitton purse that I paid for with my saved change, the one Dad thought I was ridiculous for paying $100 for—if he only knew.

We were typical sisters, with moments that did not highlight our better attributes. But, we loved each other like crazy, and God help you if you dare say anything about either one of us to the other. Marion has my back, and I have hers, always. Our story is still being written, and she still influences me like no other.

Her journey took an unexpected turn this year. And yet, Marion is still the example of how to navigate your world turning upside down with grace and dignity. She still looks out for me amid her grief. Her courage has reached new heights and she is an example of digging deep within yourself to find the strength to carry on. She is my hero, the one who leads by example, who has made tapping into your power an art form.

My sister played the most significant role in activating all these lessons I have learned from the generations before me. She is the one who motivated me to use them and convinced me to stop being a victim of my own judgments of myself. She handed me my big girl pants and made me choose my path—the one where I had to find my belief and the control to make things change.

I had a choice! Who knew?! With a lifetime of lessons, influences, and a good, swift kick in the pants, the power was there. It all leads me to my courage. I took all of it to jump into my uncertainty and grow into the person I am now.

I borrowed the different lessons in courage from these remarkable women. They impressed upon me to do all the things that were necessary to become a contributing member of my community and to advocate for children, to raise a family and face everything that comes along with it, and to take control of my family's financial health by opening my own business.

My husband (and I) experienced seven layoffs in five years.
You could say it was a stressful time in our life. We had four
young daughters, a mortgage, and debt, the kind that comes from
unexpected expenses like car repairs and emergency plane tickets.
We were just like any other family. But, one thing changed with
that last layoff. I could never let my family be that vulnerable
again. I had to find a way to take that power back. It was the final
piece of the puzzle I needed to take things into my own hands.
Now I was a businessperson—the founding partner of a physical
therapy office.

What did I know about running a business? I have been a stay-
at-home mom for years. That, my friends, was my training. My
volunteer positions and all the hats I wore running a household
provided my basics. But, it was time to take another leap. We
opened in 2000 and have survived so many obstacles, including
a pandemic. Whether I am talking to a patient or strongly
encouraging insurance companies to see things my way, I have to
tap into my courage every day.

When I jumped into this endeavor, I no longer needed to borrow
from my role models. This time, I had my own courage to work
with. As a result, I finally began finding my worth and my
potential. I can accomplish anything I set out to do because I have
everything I need within me. I promise you, you do too! Finding
this empowerment fuels my ambition every day.

Role models are not just for young folks. I drew from people
within my world, but you do not have to. Model on anyone who
owns the characteristics you believe you need to be courageous. It
could be a character in a movie or book. They can be an actor or
actress. They can be an author or any person that influences you.
Who are the people you admire? Who has the characteristics of
the person you want to be? Find them and go for it. Go after your
potential with the courage that lives inside you.

I will not tell you the insecurities do not pop back up, because they do. I face challenges every day. The difference now is that I have the tools to put my fear aside. Even when it came to authoring this book. I was so honored, but just two minutes later, asked John if I would screw it up! So, my newest big girl pants are on as we travel through creating this miracle of a publication together. We are human, old habits die hard, and we are not defined by our patterns.

Be willing to rise to any challenge, to take risks. You are already showing courage every time you step out, do something different, or talk to new people. It takes courage to put yourself out there. It takes courage to go to work, and to volunteer. You are putting yourself in a position to be judged.

It takes courage every time you leave your home, every time you go to a store and interact with people.

It takes courage to marry and have a family. Put faith in your ability to care for and nurture those you love most.

Furthermore It takes courage to love—the ultimate vulnerability of putting your heart at risk. I would venture to think that most people would not believe that these practical, everyday efforts are acts of courage, and yet they are.

As these gestures grow in frequency, you will notice that your belief in your abilities and confidence will grow along with them. You are standing in your power, in your ability to accomplish anything you set your sights on.

There it is; you have it inside you. You have everything you need.

"You are the miracle you've been waiting for."

~ Unknown

CHAPTER TWO

Nothing Is Possible Without Courage; Courage Is a Muscle

By John Spender

Miracles find you when you step up and out of your comfort zone. Nothing magical happens without the courage to dream bigger than you ever imagined, taking action to bring it all together.

A few years ago, I was sitting on the toilet seat with the lid down, wearing board shorts and staring at the grey contemporary tiles in my outdoor bathroom in Sanur, Bali. The neighbor's ten or so birds were chirping away in their mango tree that grew over part of the bathroom, providing shade. I was preparing myself to record my first ever breathing meditation. My feet were flat on the floor on the large tiles mixed with volcanic stones in between, trying not to drop my mobile phone from my shaking hand. I hit the record button.

We were getting ready to launch book three in the A Journey of Riches series: *Making Changes.* I was collaborating with twelve other authors from six different countries on this project. Part of the book launch was to have each co-author give a gift, so when readers downloaded the book, they would receive additional value. We made it even more challenging by not allowing anyone to give away a free coaching session, as half of the authors in the book were coaches. As part of the launch, readers were also getting a copy of the first two books. It was a challenge to think of what I could gift that would add value to the readers.

When you are productive, I think it is advantageous to break up your production cycles with some form of activity. I find it helps to maintain a healthy state of mind throughout the day. I have been meditating for many years now, and I've developed my own breathing technique. This style only takes about 11 minutes and creates a blissful state of clarity. I had only really used it for myself and had never thought about sharing it with the world. Once I came to grips and got over myself, I came to the understanding that this gift could make a difference in someone else's life. That gave me the courage to record the meditation while keeping my ever-present nerves under control.

I played back the recording and I chuckled with surprise at how good it sounded. Especially with the neighbor's birds naturally chirping in the background. A few months later—after a successful book launch, receiving #1 honors in a bunch of countries—one of my co-authors, Casey Plouffe, contacted me after using the meditation. She requested that I teach it at her retreat in the States later in the year.

> **"When you go out of your comfort zone and it works, there's nothing more satisfying."**
> ~ Kristen Wiig

More often than not, we are rewarded when we summon the courage to leave our comfort zones for the greater good of humanity. This is one of the best win/win scenarios you can experience. Fear and trepidation are replaced with confidence and a justified sense of elevation. There is so much personal growth to experience when we choose the courageous path. When we take a chance on ourselves and dare to risk it all, defying the illusion of safety. Let's face it, nothing is possible without courage.

In his book, *Secrets of the Millionaire Mind*, T Harv Ecker recommends patting yourself on the back and telling yourself, "It's okay; you're growing," any time you go outside your comfort zone and move towards your dream. Having done almost all of Harv's trainings, I've personally heard him share that when he sets goals, no matter how small, he pats himself on the back and says: "Well done, Harv! You did well." This anchors the goal into his subconscious mind. I learned this principle from my days of teaching Christopher Howard's NLP trainings in Singapore. Self-praise is necessary for increased personal growth, and that's why positive self-talk is a valuable and rare character trait. Celebrating your wins, no matter how small, is one of the most effective ways to fast-track and maintain high levels of self-esteem. When practiced consistently, it primes our courage muscle.

Say Yes to Opportunities That Scare You

There I was, in the States with Casey. We had just experienced Sedona with another friend and had the best time trekking through the park. Which included an epic helicopter ride. I was feeling a little nervous about teaching the breathing technique that I created. Casey had told another friend how amazing my breathing meditation was, and he wanted me to lead a session with the speakers of his retreat in St. George, Utah. Naturally, I said yes, trusting that everything would work out.

I had time to sit with the idea as our hiking guide took us through the incredible red rock formations and showed us ancient Native American rock paintings. It was here that Casey suggested that I do a breathing session. When I agreed, I didn't tell her that this would be my very first time doing it with a group, even though there was just the four of us. I was nervous but considered it good practice before the first retreat a few days from then in Utah.

Our session was located at an ancient site high up the side of the mountain with views of the rocky, tree-lined valley. During the session, a gust of wind came from nowhere and suddenly stopped. It felt like the magical presence of spirit reminding us that we were

21

on sacred grounds. It became a topic of conversation afterward. Each of us was feeling grateful, realizing what a privilege it was to be hiking in this protected area closed to the general public. I was naturally on cloud nine, brimming with confidence after stepping into the unknown and flexing my courage muscle.

Personally, I feel there is a common global misconception in society about what it means to be courageous. At least in the countries where I have traveled. It may be different in various indigenous cultures. Most people think that you have to do a heroic act to be considered courageous. In my view, anyone who steps outside their comfort zone in pursuit of his or her passion is an everyday hero. Cemeteries around the world are filled with people who didn't live their love, chose not to go for their dreams, and didn't take a chance on themselves to create a better reality for all that walk this Earth. Courage allows us to get outside our comfort zones and do the things that bring us joy while in service to others.

I was going to collate an anthology book about getting outside of your comfort zone called *Everyday Heroes,* but I was unable to generate enough interest. I received push back from potential writers stating they didn't feel comfortable being portrayed as a hero. People generally don't consider overcoming everyday fears as heroic.

"It takes courage to grow up and become who you really are."
~ E. E. Cummings

The drive from Sedona to St. George, Utah was a long one. We felt grateful to have arrived safely after narrowly missing a deer that sprinted across the road. After a day of filming for my soon-to-be released movie documentary, *Adversity,* we went hiking with a healer friend of Casey's on one of the many nature reserves in the area. After a few hours of walking into a pretty canyon, Casey suggested I take everyone through my breathing meditation. I took this as another opportunity to practice before the event. Again, the feedback was very positive. The more I shared my technique, the more I shed my fear of not being good enough. This allowed me to let go of my imposter syndrome.

Be Resourceful

Sir Richard Branson is famous for his saying: "If someone offers you an amazing opportunity and you're not sure you can do it, say yes—then learn how to do it later!" After reading many of Branson's books, I have discovered that one of his main strengths was his ability to create favorable outcomes out of nowhere. For example, the time he and his wife, Joan, were at some airport in the Caribbean and their flight was canceled. Thinking outside the box, Branson inquired about chartering a plane. The cost was something like 30,000 USD, and he drew up a sign stating: "Charter flight to the US—tickets $10,000 each." He sold eight seats, pocketing around $50,000 for his troubles.

I was inspired by another story in his book, *Losing My Virginity*. Richard and Virgin Records were putting on a sold-out concert for Mike Oldfield's Tubular Bells. The problem was, Mike was known as an introvert. He suddenly got cold feet and pulled out at the last minute. This would have been a disaster for Richard, costing Virgin Records hundreds of thousands of dollars in refunds, on top of the bad publicity.

Branson knew that he needed to treat the situation delicately or Oldfield would go into hiding. Over the phone, he supported Mike's decision to withdraw from the sold-out concert and invited Mike over for a drive in his red '78 MG convertible. Branson suggested that Mike drive, and they went through the countryside talking about anything but the concert.

On their return to Richard's house, he suggested to Mike that if he did the concert that night, he could keep Branson's sports car. Mike thought about it for a moment and agreed. The next day, the London papers reported that it was a performance of a lifetime and the concert received rave reviews. It was Branson's courage to be resourceful and take a different approach that saved the day.

Where in your life are you faced with a seemingly insurmountable challenge? And how can you play it to your advantage, for the greater good of all?

I arrived at the Follow Your Bliss retreat early to take the leadership team through my mini breathwork session. Comprised of about 12 people, we went on an 11-minute journey together. The positive feedback I received from everybody was just the boost that I needed. I was invited to speak the next day about developing my vision for the film I had written and produced. To my surprise, the audience was transfixed by my every word and—feeling inspired—a few audience members bought the A Journey of Riches books and asked for my autograph. It was a surreal experience birthed from a breathing meditation I did in my outdoor bathroom while sitting on the toilet seat. The synchronicities that followed were incredible and beyond my wildest imagination. I couldn't have planned the sequence even if I'd wanted to. As they say in the spiritual community, let go and let God.

"Courage is not the absence of fear, but rather the judgment that something else is more important than fear."
~ Ambrose Redmoon

Spending a relaxing few days with Casey and her husband, Mike, at their lakeside home in Fayetteville, North Carolina, was the perfect way to process the previous week and mentally prepare for her five-day You Can Have It All retreat in Hilton Head, South Carolina. This retreat was, as expected, another fantastic experience of being surrounded by positive people who all wanted to improve their lives on some level. I was running a breathwork session every morning as the sun came up over the ocean, plus sessions in the evenings as well. The breathing sessions were a highlight of the retreat for many of the 50-odd people in attendance. I kept getting requests for a recording, and so, I made a YouTube video of my breathing meditation for everyone that attended the retreat. You can watch it here: https://www.youtube.com/watch?v=WONeBxakezI&t=180s. I hope you allow this free recording to take you to a state of bliss. If you can get into the habit of listening to it every morning before you begin the day, you'll delight in watching the synchronicities flow into your life.

Meeting the skilled and talented trainer, Rod Hairston, was another highlight of the retreat. Rod led the retreat for the last two days. He is a high-performance coach, motivational speaker, and author and his online trainings are legendary in the personal development industry. We got on well, although I was in awe whenever I was in his presence. He sat down next to me at a restaurant in town on the last night of the retreat and asked what I did. He suggested a collaboration between us. I told him about my film, and in the next minute, we were hashing out the details of a film shoot in his home just outside Austin, Texas.

Filming Rod was both a challenging and insightful experience. It was challenging in that Rod had assured me that he had a mini studio in his home where they recorded all the company online training videos. However, it turned out that their camera wasn't a 4k video recorder, so at the last minute, I had to look for something else. We only had a small window for recording, because Rod had to facilitate training in Michigan and I had a return flight to Bali, Indonesia. I had a green screen that I traveled with, and Rod's team had excellent lighting and a boom mic. We just needed a high-quality camera.

I was in a panic and I was calm at the same time. You see, I had been in this situation before and my go-to resource was thumbtack.com. It's an online version of the yellow pages, featuring all kinds of services that you can hire. We needed someone who could show up and film the next day. Scouring the site for someone who would work on such short notice, I ended up with two quotes from videographers. The work of one of the videographers looked really good. He responded to my messages quickly and the shoot was booked. As easy as that, or so I thought.

When he arrived on the day of the shoot, he didn't have the camera we had agreed upon. He stank of cigarettes and alcohol, but at least he was on time. It turned out the camera he had was much better, but I wasn't sure if the color would match the rest of the footage we already had. When you chose courage over fear, it doesn't mean you won't have challenges. However, it shifts you to an empowered mindset that allows you to deal with them as they arise.

**"Courage is the commitment to begin
without any guarantee of success."**
~ Johann Wolfgang Von Goethe

Having a front-row seat and asking Rod questions as he stared down the barrel of the lens was a magical experience. In no time at all, the shoot was done. The videographer had assured me that the footage would be outstanding. He agreed he would color-code it to the existing footage that I had. He was also willing to wait for payment so I could check with my editor as well. During the setup, I knew he was good just by the way he thought while navigating the space we had for the shoot.

Everything worked out in the end, and to think that shoot came about from me deciding to record and share a breathing meditation. Naturally, my month in the States wasn't without challenges, but they were fun challenges to overcome. It requires some resourcefulness and a good support network, and you won't always feel ready; but when you take the leap of faith, more often than not, your wings appear. Of course, it also helps when the people around you want to see you succeed.

One of my favorite up-and-coming directors, James Cullen Bressack typifies the courage it takes to follow your vision. James comes from a family that has made its mark in the movie industry.

His dad, Gordon, is an Emmy Award-winning writer, and his mom, Ellen, is a voice actress.

Although he only lasted one month in film school, James has gone on to direct or produce more than 45 Hollywood films, including *Fortress, Survive the Game, Above the Law,* and many more. He shot his first movie on an iPhone with a budget of only $7,000. Not long after he walked out of film school, he received a call from the cafe where he worked part time and was asked to go in to work. When Bressack explained to the owner that he was making a movie, the owner told him that he needed to decide whether he was going to make low-budget films or earn real money. James used that conversation as motivation, and he went as far as getting the word *life* tattooed across his knuckles. The logic is that he wouldn't be able to get a regular job with a tattoo on his hand. Now, every time he looks down, he's reminded of what he set out to do. Today, at age 29, Bressack is one of the youngest prolific filmmakers in Hollywood.

Most of my friends who are living on purpose deliberately put themselves in situations that scare them. What do I mean? For example, if one of my friends were a successful yoga teacher and wanted to start running lifestyle retreats, they would start researching and taking public speaking classes to strengthen their presenting skills when they're not on a yoga mat. Courage is a muscle, and it is developed through use. If you can't face your fears, how will miracles find you? All too often, I feel that people fear fear.

Will Smith has said that he is motivated by fear. A reporter asked him: "What do you mean?" And I remember him saying something like: "I'm terrified by fear; anything that scares me, I do it until the fear is gone." That is a great attitude to have, and no wonder he is such a huge success today. Will recently bungee jumped out of a helicopter for his 50th birthday. Talk about facing your fears!

I'm not talking about adrenaline sports. I'm talking about everyday activities, and the actions you should be taking on a daily basis but don't. The actions that will build your business or find you your ideal partner. You really need to value the benefit of getting outside your comfort zone. One of the keys to developing courage is doing things that scare you. Another way to expand your courage muscle is to create habits that build solid foundations for your life. Being able to manage your emotions is helpful when taking healthy risks. You start by building the foundation the moment you wake up. If you can win the first hour of your day, then it's easier to win the rest of your day.

**"Be brave. Even if you're not, pretend to be.
No one can tell the difference."**
~ H. Jackson Brown Jr.

In many of her interviews, the late author, poet, and civil rights activist Maya Angelou used to say: "That when she is facing the world, she is not standing alone." Maya used to imagine that all of her ancestors were standing behind her, supporting her many endeavors.

All too often, we play it too safe in the game of life. In the process, we undervalue the difference we make in the lives of others. There is something more important than fear. When you focus on what matters, you never know where life will take you. I would never have thought that recording my breathing meditation in my outdoor bathroom would result in an epic adventure around the States. Take a chance on yourself. Cemeteries around the world are filled with people who didn't take a chance on themselves.

Embrace the concept of being your own miracle by honoring your individual pace. Every step, no matter how small, signifies progress—a testament to your ability to nurture personal growth. Within this journey, you're cultivating your courage, making it stronger with each healthy risk you embrace, and stepping into the profound wisdom life offers. Instinctively follow your intuition, for at its core, it's the foundation of this transformative process, and it all begins with the courage you summon from within.

"The power to create your own miracles lies within you. It's time to unleash it."

~ Unknown

CHAPTER THREE

Abundance

By Annette Forsythe

Redefining my wealth was one of the first crucial lessons of my growth journey. I can't say I spent a lot of time thinking about my financial health other than focusing on making ends meet to support my young family.

Financial struggles plagued the household I grew up in, where the size of your bank balance determined your wealth. There was an abundance of scarcity and negative beliefs about wealth, which translated to ideas that "there was never enough" and "there would never be enough" as a kid. We couldn't do things because it cost too much money. My sister and I joked that we experienced attractions by having the exit pointed out to us. "Girls, there is the exit for South of the Border." This, of course, left me wondering why some have enough and others do not. Was this scarcity to be my destiny? I believe it comes down to perspective. If someone has more than you do, do you see that as your loss or a shortcoming? That's scarcity. If you are the one with more, is that your "win?"

By definition, abundance is a substantial quantity of something with more than enough for everyone. Think about walking into a large department store. First, you see the overflowing displays and shelves stacked high, filled with stuff. That is abundance. There is so much available that it can be overwhelming.

Money is likely your first thought when thinking about abundance, but it is only a small part. Money is the smallest detail of my thoughts when it comes to concepts such as "wealth" and "abundance."

I always marveled at how people could make things happen. How can the average family afford to take extravagant trips or vacations? Don't they live like us—paycheck to paycheck? Experience has taught me that you can make anything happen with belief and a strong focus. You have to plan and stay consistent and believe! When we manifest wealth, seeing it already occur in your vision creates a positive energy that can lead you to success and wealth creation. I no longer decline opportunities because I cannot afford them, because I know I can make anything happen. For example, my friend's son is getting married in Italy this spring. I don't know all the specific details yet, I just know that I will be there.

Once I started thinking about focus, the Laws of the Universe became part of the picture, adding a deeper meaning to the power we have within ourselves.

The Law of Abundance states that everything we need is available to us all the time. That we have an unlimited "source" of everything. Call that source your "Higher Power," "God," "Spiritual Leader," or whatever supports your beliefs. You can attract enough of anything in your life with positive thinking and gratitude.

Over the years, I have developed a strong mindset about abundance and gratitude using these laws. We have two choices: to be content and happy, or not. Those of us will just accept that we don't have enough or won't accomplish what we want. But some believe that the sky's the limit and no matter the circumstances, they will find the positive outcome that opens the door to abundance.

When the COVID-19 pandemic hit, it was such a strange time for all of us. The world was shut down, and no one really understood the complexity of what was happening around us. We were all so isolated. No one had a clue how long any of this would last. Who could have ever anticipated that two years would pass, and we would still have some of the same questions?

Every time I would feel overwhelmed about circumstances, my gratitude would remind me of the abundance in my life, which would calm me down. There wasn't anything I could control about the shutdown, but I could control how I responded to my fear and uncertainty. I chose to focus on what was good in my life, even though it felt like everything was falling apart. With time, the funniest thing happened. That focus brought me comfort.

The lesson here was to live in the present. There was no need to wait for something better because I already had enough to be happy. So, I kept smiling and sent the message that my cup was full. I was grateful for a good life. I found my abundance in my state of being, so there was no need to worry. This eventually left me at peace surrounded by all my blessings.

It has been my experience that when you can live with a belief of abundance in your heart, your world is richer. You can see your environment through different lenses, you aren't held back by scarcity. It opens the door to thinking of others and what you can do for them. I don't mean handing over a check (although sometimes that can be an option). I mean offering kindness and support. The added value just comes back to you tenfold, resulting in more abundance.

Once I found the abundance in my life and eased my mental health, it was time to focus on the business. I am the founding partner of a physical therapy office, where we have been serving the public for over 22 years. I couldn't control the pandemic or its effect on my business, but I could control how I showed up and put my best foot forward.

When the reality of COVID hit New Jersey, we didn't know where these circumstances would lead us. We followed every report so closely; everyday findings seemed to get more serious. Were we heading for a shutdown? I thought my world was ending. I really needed to dig deep inside myself. The uncertainty was suffocating. Suddenly, my business, my income, and my security were all at risk. There was not one thing I could do about any of it. I was constantly reminding myself that I could control my actions. Grasping for answers, I had to find my belief first. Once I could reel in my anxiety, I did another inventory of my life. We had a roof over us, we had the equipment we needed, we had a customer base, we had our health, and we still had jobs. Abundance.

We kept hearing about how the virus affected different populations. Treating a mainly senior population, most of our patients were considered high-risk. Suddenly, we were canceling appointments for our high-risk patients, and one by one, we were putting them on hold until it would be safe for them to resume treatments. Our numbers were dwindling and so was our income. Then, in one day, we received not one but three calls from patients that had been directly exposed to COVID.

Okay, this nightmare was now starting to hit a bit too close to home. They had all just been in the office, indirectly exposing all of us who worked there. Since we were running a medical clinic, we had to protect everyone, staff and patients alike. So we decided to close for two weeks to get through the incubation period. It was crushing, but it was the responsible thing to do. We all walked out of the office that day in disbelief and fear and expecting to see each other in two weeks.

My emotions were all over the place. The business was not going to survive. We were done! Dramatic, I know, but very real at the moment. I did not want to play. Imagine if we had known that two weeks would end up as two months. The world shut down the following Monday. Now what?

The office had been through scary times before, and we always prevailed. I had to believe we would prevail this time too. But two weeks turned into two months, elective surgeries had stopped, and we were forced to lay off our entire staff. My business partner and I were the last two standing. We had homework to do. What was next? My answers were there, starting with my belief. We were not going to fail. We did too much good in this world for it all to fall apart now. Nope, we were survivors. We still had work to do.

By the nature of our insurance reimbursements, income continued to come in for three weeks. I had continued to go into the office to keep up with any remaining office work. I was there alone, and I knew I would be safe.

At this point, you are probably wondering what any of this has to do with abundance. The belief and conviction that there would be enough money and work to keep us going were rooted in abundance. And we did keep operating by the grace of God and the federal government.

They say misery loves company, and it was indeed comforting to know we were not the only small business in this position. Small businesses, the cornerstone of the economy, were all taking a big hit. Unemployment was surging, and a plan to keep employees on the payroll emerged. We got through the first month without pain. Our income was drying up, we were shut down, and we still had responsibilities. Our regular expenses like rent and utilities did not stop because we were shut down. Even though we were considered an essential service, physical therapy services were a gray area. By the end of the second month, I did not know how to pay the rent, let alone all of the other bills in the stack. My belief may have waned a bit. After all, how was I going to come up with $25,000?

It was a glorious day when the phone began ringing; an emergency procedure required the patient to have aftercare physical therapy. It wasn't much, but it was a start. My business partner and I returned to work for one patient. He came for a one-hour appointment and then we spent another hour sanitizing everything afterward. The following week, another patient called and then we were seeing two patients a week. They were scheduled three hours apart, and so it began. If we were seeing just a few patients, we could start the cash flow again. A little cash flow was a lot better than no cash flow. Everyone has to start somewhere.

By June, we were slowly adding people into the schedule. It was just the two of us. The Payroll Protection Plan became available by this time, and the Small Business Association was offering disaster loans. Medicare gave grants based on your billing to them from the year before. Of course, there were restrictions on how the money was spent. The money was to be used to cover expenses that would keep your business alive. Each of these programs was a lifeline to any business struggling. Our applications were submitted as soon as the process opened. We had no idea of time frames, and details were scarce. We just had an abundance of hope, grateful that there was assistance to keep us alive.

It was a few weeks later when I walked into work on an early Monday morning. Going through my morning routine, I was elated to find that the business account had been infused with a miracle! Medicare's grant and an advance on a disaster loan magically just showed up in the account. I had no idea how figures were reached. All I cared about was that I could pay the rent and catch up on all the bills.

When we were approved for the Payroll Protection Plan, we started paying the staff and bringing them back gradually. We were safely building a patient load, scheduling them so that everyone was socially distanced and protected. The PPP covered us for three months and we would be able to bank these payments that were coming in as a foundation for when the assistance money was gone.

Netcong Physical Therapy was coming back. There were plenty of stressful days, and there were even more days that we had to acknowledge we had absolutely no control of what was happening.

Our only option was to simply keep moving forward, one step at a time. Our strong belief in what we were creating would have to be enough to keep us going.

As business partners, we faced every hurdle together with courage. We stayed informed of every update and each opportunity offered to survive. That included another round of PPP. We applied for a disaster loan and were denied because we didn't show any loss. Neither of us could understand that logic. Total income to zero, we operated at over an 82% loss that first year. Yikes! I don't know how we kept the doors open. We would have to appeal that decision and ask for a reconsideration.

Day by day, step by step, inch by inch, we just kept showing up. Finally, halfway through the second year of the pandemic, realizing we were living our new normal, we were still operating at a 50% loss of revenue. If the restrictions remained as they were, we needed more staff and especially more space to continue doing what we loved doing. If Netcong Physical Therapy would return to its former glory, we needed to grow to keep taking care of people in our desired fashion.

Anything can happen if you just believe it! Lots of belief, conviction, and the daily practice of gratitude. Things were definitely different, and there was nothing wrong with that. Every day brought a new opportunity and we had the courage and vision to make things happen.

COVID had dominated our lives for a little under two years. There was constant stress and daily struggles, but it ironically somehow became a very peaceful and calm time for me personally. Every day presented us with an abundance of tools to figure out the path we needed to follow. We were going to do this, and we would be successful. Netcong Physical Therapy would be restored to its best because we believed we could do it. We just needed to figure out how.

Earlier, I spoke of paying attention and being aware of the abundance around you. I am now approaching retirement, and leaving my greatest career accomplishment while it was floundering was never even a consideration. But the reality was there. Social Security and my Medicare coverage were coming whether I was ready or not. At some point, we needed that exit plan. So, my partner and I met with our advisor to begin educating ourselves on our next steps. How would I start pulling away? How creative could we get in the buyout? Are we better off selling? Can I just stay forever? It was definitely a fact-finding mission—a very emotional task. I cried through the whole meeting. This was in June 2021.

Never doubt, we are exactly where we are supposed to be at any given moment. My partner had stopped for gas on the way to work the next day. While filling his tank, he looked up to see a sign that read, "For Lease." When he arrived at the office, he asked me, "Annette, do you think you got one more adventure in you?" You are probably guessing where this is heading. I called the number on that sign. It was a brand-new building that construction had actually stalled on because of the pandemic. Now it was completed and ready to lease. I scheduled an appointment for us to see the property later that week.

Then life got exciting. We received an email from our current landlord that same evening. All the property around us had been sold to a developer and we were to be the last business standing. Primary construction materials and equipment, along with the loss of the entire parking lot, presented an insurmountable challenge. The pandemic did not put us out of business, which could certainly do the job. It seemed as if the writing was on the wall: fight or flight.

We saw the new space and were both taken in immediately. Both of us felt like it was already a done deal. We signed the lease shortly after that. Our answer to the future was now in our hands.

NPT was going to thrive because we took care of people for all the right reasons and did it safely. Once the lease was signed, the transition moved quickly. Growth was on the horizon. Let the adventure begin! Didn't it all just make sense? Who would not choose to build a renewed business in the middle of a pandemic? There were signs all over the place; this is precisely what was supposed to happen. It all fell into place over the course of a week. We had to approach it like a new business. Essentially, we were starting over. We had twice the treatment space, enough room to increase our professional staff, and no one would be crowded, just like our vision.

The renovation took about two months. We had floor plans to create, carpet samples to choose from, paint colors to pick, curtains to install, signs to order. What new equipment did we want? How did we want to create the right atmosphere? As the days passed by, we watched our dream come to fruition. Every time I stopped by to check on the progress, the gratitude in my heart grew. We moved into the new location over the course of four days. Packing on Friday, movers on Saturday, setting up on Monday, and our first patients on Tuesday, October 5, 2021. Again, everything fell into place. We were tired, happy souls, content in knowing this was the answer to our prayers. This was the future; we had planted the seeds and the harvest would be sweet and abundant.

Now that we were in our new home, it was time to get to work. Scheduling went back to four patients an hour, and we still had enough treatment space for when we brought another therapist in. The schedule was growing. We were even working off a waiting list. It was apparent that it was time to grow the professional staff.

This was a straightforward search. We knew we wanted someone who would like to practice and be here as much as we did. We were confident that we would find the perfect match. In the past, our hiring efforts always felt like a fire drill, needing to fill the position immediately. This time, however, was different. We created an environment where the staff and patients wanted to be there as much as we did, not because they had to.

Resumes filtered in, interviews happened, and we stuck to our strategy. Our chosen candidate brought experience, energy, and a full-circle moment. She had been one of our aides when she was in high school! The new energy was palpable. There was laughter and hard work. People were being taken care of. Our sense of community had been restored.

But the journey isn't over, and we are still building a schedule, knowing we are well on our way. Belief in abundance has kept this adventure moving forward. I see as I move forward toward my retirement, this business will have everything it needs to thrive and carry on my legacy.

I know this has been a long tale, but I hope you will realize that a belief in abundance drove every step. I have never thought for a moment that our new vision would fail. Just like planting seeds in a garden, dreams take time to grow.

The moral of the story is simple. Pay attention, look around you, be grateful for the abundance you have, and know there is plenty more where that came from. You can conquer any adversity when you realize there will always be enough.

As we go through the virtues in this book, you will see that they are all built on each other. You need a part of all of them to be your greatest self. For example, in my business, I needed courage, belief, and abundance. The gifts this business has given me in return are too many to count. Not only has it allowed me to keep a roof over my family's head for many years, but it has also given me the most incredible relationships in my life. Friendships that I will cherish and encounters I will never forget. Not only have I been able to make a difference in people's lives, but they have also had a significant impact on mine. Abundance! What you give, you get back in return!

One of the greatest gifts I have ever received from my job was to personally be there for one of our patients. We had known this gentleman for many years, as his mom had been one of our original patients. They both had such complicated health histories, and they were a fantastic team as they looked out for one another. As the years passed and they grew older, the mother grew more dependent on her son, challenging his ability to care for her. They only had each other; their family was not close by. The little town we are in knows how to look after their own and this man was beloved by everyone who knew him. We lovingly called him the "mayor" because he walked all over town and knew everyone. Our office was always safe for him, even when he was not a patient. Daily visits were not unusual, and we always had good snacks!

It was not an unusual occurrence for his mom to be taken to the hospital, but things were going to be different on this occasion. His mom's sudden inability to walk or use her hands was going to change everything. She would not be returning home anytime soon. So, my sweet innocent friend was on his own. When he found out his mother would not be returning home, he came to us for help, and that is exactly what we did.

There were trips to his doctor and trips to the grocery store. There were lessons about cleanliness and hygiene, and he would bring his laundry to us to be washed. We do our linens at the office, so one extra load a day wasn't an issue. My partner and I covered a spending account at a local diner (his favorite), so we knew he would get a hot meal every day. My business partner took care of his haircuts and shaved him when his beard got crazy. We just did anything that could support him, so that he didn't feel alone or scared.

When the season changed, I made sure he had warm clothes and I even made sure we had a little treat for him each week, usually coloring books and crayons or some toy. Halloween was his favorite holiday. I took him shopping for his costume and some decorations. He wanted to be a scary monster and so we shopped until he found every detail. There was just so much innocence. How could I not make sure his costume was perfect?

There was a nurse liaison at the rehab center who assisted me in setting up FaceTime calls to talk to his mom. I was compelled to do anything in my power because I just did not want him to feel lost. His sister lived in California; she was going through everything that needed to be done so that she could take him home with her, allowing me to handle our end while she did what was required.

We knew his mom was not coming home and would become a permanent resident at the nursing home by this point. My friend went to their apartment to get her belongings. It was so tiny. She had so little, it broke my heart. More shopping was needed, so I went out and got some sweatpants, PJs, and warm socks so that she could be cozy. It's what I would have done for my own mom if she needed things. I could not let this woman lie in a bed in clothes that did not fit her. We would send her pictures and I would help her son write letters. They just both missed each other so much.

Long story short, he could go with his sister. Leaving his mom was hard, but he had adjusted beautifully. He is now thriving in his new community and they continue to stay connected with me. Every time I hear his voice, I am reminded of how lucky I was to share the experience with him. I could help and never once worried about it being too much. I am the lucky one.

This is how you feel when you live with an abundant mindset. There is always enough to go around, to make a difference. Like I said at the beginning of this chapter, I am one of the wealthiest people in the world! My life is blessed.

"Miracles occur naturally as expressions of love. The real miracle is the love that inspires them."

~ A Course in Miracles

CHAPTER FOUR

See It Everywhere

By John Spender

To be self-reliant is to be in alignment with the abundance that is all around you. It's a way of being, and it starts with feeling abundant. I'm talking about an embodiment of empowerment, a state where you become so self-sufficient that your surplus of energy, wealth, and prosperity goes to helping others in desperate need. For example, in the A Journey of Riches book series, the royalties go to charity, primarily to support the disabled and elderly in Bali, an island with a special place in my heart. We launched the series in 2015 and have released 27 titles to date, raising 13,000 dollars or 130 million in Indonesian rupiah, which can go a long way in a developing country. Being self-reliant is one's ability to connect with abundance. It's about giving just as much as it is about receiving wealth into your life. Ultimately, it is through giving that we receive.

The law of reciprocity is a balanced exchange between giving and receiving. It's a form of giving that serves and empowers the recipient just as much as the giver. In Wallace Wattles' book *The Science of Getting Rich*, he called it equal, fair exchange. For instance, he stated that if a trader gave an expensive antique painting to an Eskimo in exchange for some furs, the trader isn't engaging in fair exchange because the painting is of no use to the Eskimo. The same goes for our own life; giving equal or greater value than we receive keeps us in harmony with the law of reciprocity. So, if you don't have enough to give in terms of material wealth, start with giving more of your energy to others and notice yourself begin to feel more abundant.

Knowing and feeling abundant is the shield that will protect you from the limiting beliefs that everyone encounters sooner or later. Thoughts like: *Money doesn't grow on trees. We can't afford it. Do you think I'm made of money? You have to work hard for money. Money is the root of all evil. Rich people are criminals. You have to have money to make money. Who do you think I am, Rockefeller?* Do any of these thoughts sound familiar? The fear of not being abundant is passed down from generation to generation all over the globe. So many people constantly worry about how they will pay the rent. They ask themselves questions like: *Why can't I get a better job? Why can't I earn more money? Why can't I be successful? Why can't I get ahead? Why am I always broke?* These disempowering questions only reinforce the "lack" paradigm that most of us find ourselves in at some point in time. But do we want the solution? Are we keen to do something about it? Who is looking for the answer? Do we want to break the paradigm of lack, limitation, and poverty that has plagued many of our families for centuries?

Who wouldn't say yes, right? Over the following pages, I will share principles that I have learned which have guided me to live life abundantly in service to the law of reciprocity. If you apply them, you will tap into the source of abundance as surely as the night turns into day. Maybe you already have a lot of money, but you don't feel like you have enough, or you fear losing it. These feelings are opposite sides of the same hamburger. Living abundantly isn't something that comes naturally for most people. When my parents separated when I was just five years old, my mom found herself with three little people to care for, clothe, and feed. This was a huge challenge, and she responded by working hard and saving. After living on our grandparents' farm for a year, we moved into a house with holes in the floorboards and wore second-hand clothes from The Salvation Army. From the outside looking in, things may have seemed bleak, but we were okay.

Our grandparents had bought us three kids a Disney plaster mold kit which consisted of Mickey Mouse, Donald Duck, and Goofy.

My brother, being the eldest, poured the molds with the plaster and, when set, would take the molds off and paint them. The tricky part was taking the molds off. Adam was good at handling Mickey and Donald, but Goofy's nose would always break off at this delicate moment. Once we had several painted statues, we set up a table in front of our rental house on the footpath of the main road. Our first business was ready to roll. At six years of age, with blond hair and blue eyes, I was good at charming old ladies. They thought I was cute and would buy one of the Disney characters. In less than two hours, I had sold all of our stock. I wanted to repeat the process and purchase more plaster, but my elder brother bought lollies and slime-o instead. Although our first business didn't last long, I learned a valuable lesson about creating value and abundance being a state of mind. As children, we didn't see ourselves as poor or different from anyone else. Instead, we saw an opportunity, tapped into our resourcefulness, and money couldn't wait to jump into our pockets—or my brother's pocket, at least.

Abundance is all around us once we notice its presence. At that point, the limitless supply becomes more accessible. Spreading this awareness is what my fellow author Annette and I plan to do with this book. Let's share an understanding of abundance throughout the world like wildfire, a fire that will banish fear, lack, and want from your life. This awareness is the source of success, wealth, empowerment, and giving—yes, giving, because if you aren't abundant, it's difficult for you to give. Abundance is omnipresent and so powerful, magnetizing everything in your life to vibrate in harmony with it, dispelling every unwanted condition. If you are lost in a maze of false beliefs, this idea will show you the way out. If you are financially down on your luck, it will reach down and pick you up. If your faith is weak, it will fortify your resolve.

Aligning your attitude with abundance will amplify your income, attract opportunities, stimulate business, nourish your aspirations, clarify your vision, generate peace, heal wounds, remove blocks, dispel fear, squash worry, shut down doubt, raise your self-esteem,

dispel tensions, and open the doors to a new way of living. This
energy is your Aladdin's lamp to infinite abundance in every area
of your life. This isn't some sort of a-ra-a rally or exaggerated
motivational speech. I'm speaking from experience, having
lived through many ups and downs. I've had an on-and-off-
again relationship with abundance almost all of my life. I started
expanding my online coaching practice into Singapore, hosting
live events every month. I lived in Bali and barely made enough
money to cover my flights, accommodation, and expenses. I was
in fair exchange, but I didn't believe in my abilities; the venture
lasted a year before I had to admit defeat and cut my losses.

I had lost my connection with abundance consciousness and
found myself downgrading in Bali, which was quite embarrassing
for me to face and sit with my failure. It was challenging to feel
abundant when the outside world was telling me that I wasn't.
To lift myself out of this state, firstly, I developed a vigorous
morning routine consisting of yoga, affirmations, meditation,
and fresh fruits for breakfast. This helped me shift the way I saw
my reality with a primary focus on income-producing activities.
After reading Napoleon Hill's *Think and Grow Rich*, I also gave
myself ample time to daydream, creating a vision board, and I
formed my own council to confide in. An idea came to me of
making a film, which seemed crazy, as I had no money at the
time. I modeled Hill's success of having imaginary conversations
with his council. As he had indicated, the conversations I was
having started to feel real, almost like a form of telepathy. I
began to feel more abundant when one of my nightly imaginary
conversations with Dr. Michael Beckwith felt unbelievably
accurate. I explained the vision for the documentary film to the
council, and Michael spoke up as if he were in the room with me.
It was almost like a shout when he said he loved the vision and
wanted to feature in the film. I asked him, "How?" His response
was short and simple and filled me with confidence: "Come over
to Agape (his center), and we will make it happen."

I repeated the affirmation "I am abundance." I planned to reach out to as many thought leaders in the personal development space as I could and offer them a spot in the film with the promise of securing some big names like Dr. Michael Beckwith and Jack Canfield. I raised enough money to fly myself and a videographer to Los Angeles, filming Beckwith, Jack Canfield, Lisa Garr, Dr. John Demartini, and more guests over four years. I'm now on the last stretch of funding the live-action scenes.

This experience taught me that thoughts are seeds that come to us from anywhere and everywhere as they float through the air, looking for the right mental soil. The suitable ground is a part of our awareness. Just as a vegetable garden must be free from weeds to thrive, our minds need to be free from negativity, contradictory thoughts, and limiting beliefs to succeed in connecting with and becoming abundance. The problem is not with the seed but with the soil. We must remove the impediments of fear, worry, and doubt, and then the idea of abundance can take root and grow to maturity. The unseen becomes seen, starting from nothingness and rising to the manifested. Cultivating the soil of the heart, mind, and soul takes us from lack and moves us into the fertile grounds of prosperity and abundance.

So, to begin with: do you know what you desire? Do you know what you deserve? A new apartment? More money or better health? Well, plant your idea into the fertile medium of the subconscious. Plant it deep and cultivate it with recognition and belief, fertilize it with focus and concentration, and nurture it with faith and appreciation, all while activating it with your consciousness. If you condition your beingness, there is nothing that you can't bring into existence. You are an unlimited being that can create anything that you desire.

You are the universe, and the universe is you. When you enter the universe's consciousness, connecting with its intelligence, you effectively tap into all that is and ever was created. The channeler

Esther Hicks communicates this through the entity Abraham, using the term to enter the *vortex of creation*. Jesus calls it the Kingdom of Heaven. Suppose we abide in this abundance consciousness and expand our awareness, keeping our thoughts pure and our beingness true to its frequency. Simply allow the divine substance to momentarily shape itself around your thoughts as they materialize into your life in those things you think and focus on. Moreover, you must keep your mind off your troubles and center on the universal intelligence of pure consciousness—abundance consciousness.

It served me well to repeat the affirmation: "I am abundance." I invite you to say the words and truly feel them with your heart. Stake your claim and know your worth. Think "abundance" throughout the day, for that which you honor with your thoughts will be honored. Think "plenty" all the time and watch it manifest in your life in all its forms. Ralph Waldo Emerson said, "Man is what he thinks about all day long." See abundance in the flowers and the rows of stacked shelves filled with endless goods. See it in the night sky with the bountiful stars shining bright. Feel it in nature through magnificent trees. At any given moment, we are surrounded by abundance. Can you see it?

What is your main focus? Your thought pattern is the matrix through which all other thoughts pass. Worry usually starts as a slight fear in the mind and becomes cemented in one's consciousness through habitual repetition. We repeat the same worry day after day until it becomes a habit or an automatic expression. These habits of mind make a channel or a path along which all our thoughts travel. The channel enlarges as the habit is repeated, getting deeper and wider until the habit influences all our thoughts, actions, and beingness. This is why we are what we think about all day long. If someone's basic thought foundation is worry, everything in his life will be tainted by the specter of anxiety. As long as someone carries this frequency of anxiety, they will repel their goodness instead of attracting it.

You've heard about the atmosphere of homes, restaurants, buildings, towns, and communities being made up of the collective consciousness of the people who live there. A man's consciousness is related directly to the thoughts, beliefs, and habits that reveal him to others. If his primary thought is poverty or lack, others will know it and treat him accordingly. When I began to surround myself with the imaginary council of thought leaders, people like Jack Canfield, Michael Bernard Beckwith, Tony Robbins, Dr. Wayne Dyer, Lisa Garr, Alan Cohen, Rhonda Burn, Dr. John Demartini, and many more, their pictures stuck to a vision board, my consciousness began to shift. The synchronicities related to my desires manifested quickly. I mentioned earlier that the imaginary conversations felt real after consistent meetings with my committee. I spoke to a friend's husband about what I was doing. Casually mentioning the vision for the film project, he told me that he knew Jack Canfield and Dr. John Demartini and he would be happy to make an introduction. That's when the music from *The Twilight Zone* sounded in my head.

How then should we approach and change these established, destructive habits of mind? We choose to embrace a generous being towards all life, fully embodying and adapting the new paradigm we wish to create. Let's fill our awareness with thoughts of assurances, poise, faith, self-confidence, serenity, and inner determination. Allow yourself to transform by surrounding yourself with an atmosphere of success, achievement, and strength of character. Permit yourself to radiate qualities of fearlessness, inner peace, trust, optimism, and self-reliance. When we do this, we attract the best from everybody, and synchronicities become the norm. Before you know it, you will inspire confidence and compel attention. Believing in yourself will inspire confidence in others. This paradigm shift will release universal intelligence into consciousness and change your life's color, character, and tone. Instead of worry, you will generate faith. This is precisely what happened to me, and it can work for you too. Living abundantly is indeed a mindset, a way of being that anyone can embody and champion.

The question is: how do we bring our attention to what is required instead of what we believe we lack? For example, when I lost faith and trust in my abilities during my Singapore venture, I slipped into a pattern of thinking that there wasn't enough money to make things happen when, in fact, the missing ingredients were self-belief and innovation to create something different. Having a sense of awareness was the first step in changing my point of focus. This, in turn, allowed me to change my habitual thinking. Habits move along the lines of least resistance, as Edward E. Beals highlights in his book, *The Law of Financial Success,* when he states, "If you have to walk over a field or through a forest, you know how natural it is for you to choose the clearest path over the less worn one. And greatly in preference to stepping out across the field or through the woods to form a new path."

Patterns are formed through repetition and are developed by an observable, natural law. Once a piece of paper is folded in a particular way, it will naturally fold along the same lines next time. We can see this in nature as well; notice how rivers and streams cut their courses through the land and flow along effortlessly. The law of least resistance is in effect everywhere. It's like the indents in a record the needle follows. If you don't like the tune you are creating, you must scratch the record.

If we shift ourselves out of the old process of worry—the path of least resistance—we can approach life with confidence instead. As a confident thought grows, the mental path of worry will gradually fill up from disuse. The old path will grow less and less distinct until it eventually disappears. Do you see why changing habits of thought is so essential to expanding your awareness of abundance? When you know how to change your habitual thoughts, you will know how to change everything in your life. We change the world around us by changing ourselves.

In the initial phase of changing habits, allow patience, persistence, and trust to be your guiding lights. The stars don't disappear in daylight hours. We might not be able to see them, but they are still there, shining bright as in the night. You will see results when your new, conscious credo becomes deeper and more robust than the old, unconscious ones. Once the new pattern is outlined and adopted, immense certainty and confidence will take hold. Allow the idea of abundance to permeate your consciousness.

As discussed earlier, affirmations are the rock of support I needed to reshape my reality. They gave me the necessary self-confidence to birth the council for my film. I would say to myself: "I am confident. I am abundant. I am grateful. I am a success. I picture abundance for myself and others. I always have more money coming in than going out. I give generously to myself and others," and many more. Feel what you say—feel it deeply with all your heart and with great joy. Dwell on your statements until they firmly synchronize with your emotional nervous system. I follow several rules to embody new affirmations of thought and beingness.

1. Every time I caught myself using the old-habit path of lack, I celebrated the mental catch and repeated the simple affirmation that "I'm abundance and everything is always working out for me."

2. As much as I could, I kept my thoughts out of the negative path and held and affirmed positive thoughts. If you slip, celebrate and come back to your new affirmation: "I am abundance, and everything is always working out for me." Allow simplicity to be your guiding force.

3. I energized the new thought-action (affirmations) with hope, power, belief, conviction, and determination when I expressed them.

4. I made my new pattern clear, strong, profound, and as positive as possible.

5. Consistency was my secret weapon. I would repeat my affirmations three times a day to ingrain a new mental path into my subconscious mind. Repetition is the answer to forming new habits of any kind.

The objective we want to accomplish is two-fold: to eradicate the offending thought pattern of doubt and to drop a new idea into the pool of subconscious awareness so that the new, unhindered thought can take form in the creative substance that is the nucleus of abundance. The law of abundance is already within our hearts, subtly pressing the mind to act. Our job is to release it for our daily needs, to open channels for its expression.

Don't hold the idea; let the idea hold you! Do you feel me? Do not affirm unless the corresponding emotion supports your affirmation. Many people come undone at this point, but it is crucial. We display our good by earnestly connecting with the universe's intelligence, not through parroting affirmations or mouthing declarations without feeling. The law of attraction responds to us by correlating our states of mind and our hearts' essence. It operates through our mental equivalent or beliefs. If your heart isn't in it, you are not connected with the source. When the principle of abundance is set in motion through affirmation and acceptance, the law of attraction operates through us.

Why must the new thought pattern be housed in the present tense? Why do we say "I am abundance" instead of saying "I will be abundant?" Why state something we do not have? Life always works in the present moment by direct affirmation. Saying "I will be abundant" puts our abundance off until some future time. To affirm our good in the present is to cause it to appear. If the idea of abundance becomes a superpower in our lives, we must accept it as a present fact. Our thought, will, and imagination must agree with what we say. We must banish all fear of lack. For me, a turning point was loving and trusting my imagination to allow my desires to flow freely. This happened immediately after the failure in Singapore, and it began with affirmations and sitting still in meditation.

Now, I invite you to start building your basic thought pattern for abundance without further delay. Center your thought again in our affirmation, "I am abundance." This is the nucleus that grows and multiplies indefinitely. We need to back it up with persistent faith and desire. Your idea of abundance might be a better position, more income, a lovely holiday, a compatible partner, or improved health. The law of attraction says you can have anything you desire, and if you believe you already have it—that is, if you have the objective acceptance of the thing desired—then it is yours.

I invite you to reflect for a few moments. Not on the money to meet the mortgage, not on the new car, not on the new house, but on the basic idea, "I am abundance." If you accept my invitation, you're going to change your consciousness out of the old mold of lack and into the new paradigm of plenty. You will create a unique habit atmosphere, a new thought inclination, and a new state of beingness. That is your significant responsibility. We will start this idea of abundance revolving on its axis at such an elevated rate that it will draw all the good things we need to us. We will boost your consciousness to recognize monetary abundance and abundance matching any of our desires.

The rest of the process is a matter of sustained attention, faith, feeling, acting, and seeing. See a new idea, realize it, feel it, and accept it. Speed it up with your belief, keep it alive with your faith, feed it with fresh, rich, powerful life-giving images. Give it motion through action, act it out: "I am abundance." Discover how rich you are. Keep the abundance idea circulating freely through your mind. See it generating prosperity, opportunities, and success. Do not allow negative thoughts to creep in and sabotage your divine good. "I am abundance." Keep repeating it until it goes underground and takes form. "I am abundance." Feel its frequency. Rejoice in it. Bless it. Love it. Accelerate the rate of vibration by telling your subconscious mind that you are already abundant. Act with a mindset of deep appreciation.

If you desire abundance, don't say, "I want to get rid of poverty." Instead, be affirmative and positive. Say what you mean, and mean what you say. If your thoughts are filled with the idea of getting rid of lack, you are giving lack space in your consciousness. Make your primary view prosperity, opulence, plenty, and wealth. Think and speak of nothing else. Oh, yes, I know the rent is due, and you have a lot of unpaid bills, but you are not going to think of these right now. Instead, you will think abundance, know abundance, feel plenty and nothing else. You're going to etch abundance so deeply into your awareness that nothing else can come into your life. That is what we mean by building a new mental equivalent. It's creating a new thought out of impulsion that will flood your life with good. It is making a new path for God by getting everything out of her way. It takes everything that isn't perfection from out of your consciousness, trading it in for something better and more desirable.

Our desires must be definite yet flexible, and we should always expect something better than what we have set our hearts on. The purpose of our desires is to open our consciousness to its expanded form, enlarging our connection to abundance. When we start to connect with this higher consciousness, we clear the invisible channels to become visible. It is the nature of abundance consciousness to outdo itself; when our abundance is the outward growth of a rich consciousness, it is satisfying, permanent, and secure. Our job is to raise our vibration and feel worthy enough to receive.

The value of repetition cannot be emphasized enough. It's like the constant dripping of water on a stone leaving its mark. The continuous repetition of your affirmation fuses it with the subconscious mind and therefore materializes the idea. Create a timeline from your first memory of feeling abundant to the most recent one and every year in between. Allow about two hours to sit and reflect on all the plentiful moments in your life. Can you remember the first time you earned money? What about having an oversupply of food? Or your first family vacation? Recall the times when you felt most abundant and watch the increase begin to manifest into your life even more.

As you embrace the mindset of abundance, know that you are breaking generational beliefs that there is a limited supply of all things. Letting go of these limiting beliefs is like healing a virus; it takes time and determination to banish worry and welcome plenty. Seek the more rooted blessings found in giving and receiving as you become ever more self-reliant. Because it always starts with ourselves; that was true for me when I was a boy selling plaster models by the side of the road, and it was true when I was a grown man embarking on the journey of making a film and not knowing where to start. Miracles do not simply float down from the sky. They do exist, but for them to enter into our lives, we have to commit to becoming our own miracle first.

"You have within you right now, everything you need to deal with whatever the world throws at you."

~ Brian Tracy

CHAPTER FIVE

Pay It Forward

By Annette Forsythe

What is your motivation for being grateful? How do you reciprocate the kindness that comes your way? Did that kindness change the outcome of your day? You can show your gratitude by doing things for others without expecting anything in return except the confidence that the same help will come back to you when you need it.

Every time you show kindness to others, it comes back to you tenfold. Never lose sight of one important rule: we are here to serve, not be served. Pay attention and pay it forward to show gratitude for your blessed life. There is an annual Pay It Forward Day every April 28th, as well as the Random Acts of Kindness Day on February 17th. Mark your calendars!

The phrase "pay it forward" has gained popularity since the movie of the same name was released in 2000, starring Helen Hunt and Kevin Spacey—an incredible story about a young boy who was assigned a school project to come up with an idea that would influence the world. His goal? Repaying good deeds with good deeds; not paying them back. If a young boy can be this insightful, why is this such a foreign concept to many? Yet, his efforts to make a difference created a ripple of kindness, one act at a time.

Things happen to us many times in our lives, and there is no way to say thank you with reciprocation. But when you share that kind of thoughtfulness with someone else, you are paying it forward. Suppose this could be normal behavior for everyone. Yet, it has the power to change people's lives for the better and could be inspiring to those very same people to adapt.

There have been many such moments in my lifetime. Each of them has been an opportunity to show my gratitude by doing for others.

I am told I have a big heart. I am told I feel other people's emotions too deeply. I am told that I take things too personally. Here's the thing: maybe they're right. I know that in order to be true to myself, I must lead with my heart and that it makes me happy to give and do for others.

I watched my parents give of themselves throughout my childhood, even when they did not have much to offer. I was taught to be kind and always do what is right. I learned how to reciprocate the generosity of others. It was a good model. Treat others as you would want to be treated. When you are young, you do things because you were taught that way. As I grew older, I realized that it was better to do something because you chose to, because it was in your heart.

My mother passed away far too young, at 60. She went through a terrible, debilitating year before succumbing to breast cancer. I was given the most beautiful insight at that time. I watched my grandmother stay by my mother's side, gently loving and talking her through some of the hardest moments. I felt the power of the love and courage that held us up as a family.

There were so many thoughtful expressions by so many people who just wanted to support us, feed us, to help in any way possible. I had no idea how we would ever reciprocate. It was then that I realized the only way to say thank you was to carry on those good deeds for others. I have made a point of "doing this since the day my mother passed away. I vowed I would take every opportunity to serve others from then on. I committed to continue the kindness and love that we received. Some call it paying it forward, others call it acts of kindness. Call it whatever you will, it's not rocket science. It doesn't take much to be kind in many cases—the simpler the action, the bigger the impact. It doesn't have to cost a penny; you don't have to be a millionaire to make a difference.

It has become my daily practice to do one kind thing a day for no reason other than to give of myself. Pay the toll for the car behind you, or buy an unknowing soul a cup of coffee. Look someone in the eye and pay them a compliment. Sincerely ask questions about someone's well-being and truly listen to the answer. Pay a visit to someone in a nursing home. Just take any action that will brighten someone else's day. Holding a door open for someone or simply smiling can change the course of someone's day and make them feel significant.

I started by just trying to give back with my interactions with others. I have learned the importance of adding value to this world we live in. They say actions speak louder than words, and when my budget allowed, I was able to do even more. Too many people believe that you have to give money to do something good. Monetary giving is wonderful and impactful, and you can have the same effect simply by giving your heart with your actions.

When I opened my physical therapy business, my motivation came from wanting to care for my father. I lived so far away and couldn't help care for him or advocate for his health. My business was a way to do for others what I could not do for my dad. I have been blessed with the ability to care for and help ease our patients' concerns for over 22 years. It may sound so Pollyanna, but my heart is full every time I can make someone smile, hold a hand, or lend an ear. While I manage the financial end of my physical therapy practice, my daily actions at work don't cost a thing, and their impact is priceless. It's part of the experience patients have while in our care. We want every patient to feel like they are surrounded by people who care about them and their journey's outcome.

One Sunday morning, I went to the grocery store to buy a gift card. I was in the express lane. There was a lovely lady behind me. She looked as if she had just come from church. She only had a few items. The cashier was ringing up my gift card when suddenly, there was a problem with the register. I looked back and smiled; however, it did not take a moment before the woman was huffing and puffing with dissatisfaction.

Every moment she had to wait magnified her annoyance, especially when it became apparent that my purchase would take a while. I looked at her and said I was sorry to be holding her up. That this was a present for my niece and why don't we just add your items to my bill and then you can get on your way. I assured her it would be my pleasure to pay for her items to make up for the inconvenience I had caused her. The woman's whole demeanor changed. She did not know how to respond at first, and then she simply said, "Thank you, this must be my lucky day."

By this time, a line formed behind her. I smiled and apologized for delaying them and that I could not cover all their purchases. Again, I was met with laughter. Being externally focused, using an act of kindness changed the woman's entire day. Maybe she would feel enlightened enough to do something for someone she crossed paths with in the future.

Actually, being at the grocery store offers many opportunities to show goodwill. The carts at my local grocery store are locked together. It costs a quarter to release one. As often as I promise to keep a supply of quarters in the car, I am caught short regularly, as are many other patrons. So as soon as my purchases are in the car, I look for the first person I see headed toward the store and give them my cart, refusing to accept their offered quarter. I tell them it is my act of kindness for the day. I like to imagine that the cart gets passed along all day. The reward is priceless. The smile when people realize you are just being helpful warms my heart. It's a simple act with a significant effect.

It's so easy to get wrapped up in our own lives. The daily minutia can become overwhelming, and we end up in survival mode. When life gets that hectic, we forget to think about others. Our own issues get so large, we don't even register what others are going through. Was that woman's reaction really impatience, or was she worried about something? How was her health? Was someone she loved in an accident? We never know what life brings to any of the people we encounter. Either way, a simple act changed her outlook.

There was another time I was checking out, and I was behind this woman who had the most beautiful flowers, a loaf of bread, and a few other essentials. She realized she had forgotten something and ran back to get it. When she returned, she went to pay and was short of cash. The first thing she went to remove was the gorgeous flowers. Spring was here and those vibrant colors were enough to make anyone's day happy. I motioned for the cashier to just add her things to my bill. The cashier told the lady that she didn't need to worry about taking anything out because I had paid for her things. She thanked me and went on her way.

My heart had just sunk for her. The embarrassment of holding up a line and not having enough cash to cover her bill. All I felt at that moment was that I couldn't let her leave without those flowers. To my surprise, she waited for me outside the store. She explained that she had just moved, which cost her more than she thought. The cash in her wallet was all she had left until her following checks came in.

It took everything I had to hold back my tears; what the woman didn't realize was that she was the one who had given me the gift. When we parted ways, she said she hoped to pass my kindness on someday. I wouldn't call myself altruistic, I am not that nice, but I realize the more you practice kindness, the more creative you can become and the more aware you become of ways to help.

As I've already said, I am the wealthiest woman in the world. My life is filled with abundance. I am blessed. My acts of kindness come from gratitude. Every time you give, it comes back to you tenfold. I like to dream of the time when this type of thoughtfulness becomes a way of life. Imagine the ripple effect. Wouldn't you want to live in that world too?

These simple acts are powerful. When you pay it forward, you are changing someone's world. You are inspiring others to be generous and compassionate. You are creating a chain effect around kindness where all people can care about each other and look out for each other instead of focusing on themselves.

Have no doubt, there is another side to this coin. Whatever you give comes back to you. So, you are also improving your well-being and self-image, and there is a feeling of satisfaction when you know you've made a difference.

Then, there's the tricky part. You have to step out of your comfort zone. People who like to give of themselves often find it difficult to receive. However, the receiving is just as important as the giving. You must allow other people the opportunity to feel that same joy of giving. It is part of what comes back to you.

I have made benevolence a way of life. It's been my choice to keep my eyes open and look for opportunities. If you pay attention, opportunities for kind deeds are everywhere. But unfortunately, there have been times when I have been the one who has needed help. These have been extremely uncomfortable moments for me and periods of intentional growth while uncertain about my circumstances.

When my children were young, we—I should say, my husband—experienced several layoffs that were always around the holidays. I had no idea how to manage this challenge the first time it happened. Luckily, I had a strong support system of incredible friends around me. One day, my dear friend called me and said, "We're having a garage sale on Saturday at my house. Bring whatever you have to get rid of and come hang out."

There I was, completely clueless. People came and went all day long. Things were selling like crazy, and many people followed my friend in and out of her house. I thought that it was a little strange—the sale was outside. But keeping my focus on my great sales technique, I let my questions go and returned to my bartering.

After we cleaned up at the end of the day, my beautiful friends all gathered around me. Our hostess handed me a box. It was filled with checks and all the proceeds from the day. I was so overwhelmed; I couldn't believe what was happening. I am the one who is always on the other side of this exchange. I'm always the helper, not the "helpee." There are not enough words to describe my emotion and gratitude. I cried tears of gratitude; how could I be so blessed! If that wasn't enough, we went Christmas shopping the next day. When we got to the mall, she handed me an envelope. There was $1,000.00 to ensure my girls would have a happy Christmas. Sometimes, you just have to receive. My girls had a wonderful Christmas despite our circumstances.

We are not meant to be alone in this world. Sometimes, we all need help. This group of friends that I have been part of has been there for each other since we met years ago. There has been a lot of give and take, and I can't imagine my life without them.

The following year, the same thing happened yet again. This time, the layoff was in October. One afternoon, there was a knock on the door and another sweet friend was outside holding a beautiful basket filled with all the fixings for a holiday meal. The basket came from our church. I was horrified. There had to be people who needed this help more than us. I graciously accepted, tears flowing down my face. As my friend was about to leave, she handed me an envelope filled with cash from our pastor. They anticipated that we would be reluctant to accept, and we were. My husband was hired for a new position on Christmas Eve. As soon as he got his first paycheck, we donated money to help support a family whose child was in the First Communion Program. Giving and receiving are both equally humbling.

When my husband and I moved into our neighborhood, we were a young family. When winter came and the snow fell, we made sure we helped all our elderly neighbors shovel their walks and driveways. The girls would help too. You could say we have come full circle, and somehow, when I wasn't looking, we became an elderly couple. There is such comfort knowing that we are being looked after. My first response was, "No! We got this!" Then I had to graciously step back and say thank you. Once you can get over yourself, it is actually a great comfort to know you can ask for help. So, just as it is essential to create moments to give of yourself, you have to allow yourself to receive as well.

It's so odd. Sharing these stories feels like I am seeking significance. That couldn't be further from the truth. Sharing these stories shows how simple it can be that any random act of kindness can fill our needs and shed new light on our perspective.

My family has a very special "adopted" family here in New Jersey. Grateful that we were a group of adults who didn't want for anything, we decided to stop buying Christmas gifts for each other. Instead, we would use the money we would have spent to adopt a family and make their Christmas dreams come true. This is by far my most cherished Christmas tradition. We are a large group, so we always sought out a more populous family.

Once we were armed with a list of first names, ages, and a short wish list for each family member, it was time to divide and conquer. We would set out to make some dreams come true. We would split the list up between us and create magic. I wasn't shopping for a stranger, I had names and they became real in my heart as if I were shopping for my family members.

In addition to the wish list, we created a list of "essentials" that everyone had to have. Everyone needed new pajamas and slippers, new winter coats, some hot chocolate, and some special holiday treats. My girls would also do a "knitting sweatshop." All the members of the family would get handmade scarves and hats. All their knitting would happen on Thanksgiving weekend before heading back to school. Of course, the parents would never add to the wish list. And, well, you don't say no to many Italians. Everyone had presents to open on Christmas morning, including Mom and Dad.

When all was said and done, there was an abundance of gifts, decorations, and gift cards for the grocery store. Santa's elves were filled with excitement for our secret family and appreciation for everything we had in our own lives. This has been the greatest holiday joy for us for over 20 years now.

When all the shopping was done, we would pick a weekend and get together to do all the wrapping. We would present our purchases to each family member while imagining all their reactions. We would take pictures of the whole wrapping process and send them to the parents so they could feel like they were part of the process. Our gift was being together with laughter and contentment and thanksgiving.

After the work was done, we would all share a celebration meal. I do not know who got the most out of the whole experience. We truly felt we were the people receiving the gifts. Making Santa's dreams come true is quite powerful.

On a few occasions, when the families we adopted were in better financial positions, they too would become secret Christmas elves, providing them with a significant pay-it-forward moment as they came full circle. There is so much satisfaction in being able to reciprocate in any way once you have been on the receiving end of giving. Life does go full circle.

Paying it forward or random acts of kindness . . . aren't they the same thing? Both involve making the world a better place by being an unexpected pleasure for someone. Both can create a belief that you can make our world a better place. Acts of kindness can build your confidence and give you a sense of connection.

A lesson I've learned is that many people are willing to give of themselves and they don't know how to, or they don't think to. Our actions toward these unknowing people help bring awareness. They'll realize how nice it felt and hopefully think, "I can do that!" That's how the ripple starts, just one person who doesn't give up. Like the old telephone game, although it's a kind act instead of a secret, it passes on. One person tells ten people, who all tell ten people.

All these acts, random or contemplated, are more important than ever since COVID-19. They are an opportunity to restore society to a better place, away from the stress we have all been feeling. At this point, I think we could all use a little help in restoring our perspective. But unfortunately, our behavior is the only thing we can control these days.

Before you know it, you have a new way to approach a fulfilled life. There are no specific skills that are required. As previously noted, random acts of kindness are mutually beneficial. When you act with compassion, you can have an immediate internal reaction of satisfaction. These random acts teach us to be grateful for the abundance in our own lives. And the chain reaction goes both ways. The more you do for others, the more you learn to do for yourself, building a sense of belonging and reducing the feeling of being alone. You feel connected. Your well-being improves your self-esteem.

Now, I'm not a scientist and I'm certainly not a doctor. But in my opinion, compassion, kindness, satisfaction, and gratitude can equate to well-being and the joy of happiness. I would even venture to say that there are health benefits. Don't things that are good for you improve your health? Doesn't good health help you live longer? For example, living in a joyful and peaceful state can eliminate stress. Less stress eliminates inflammation and, therefore, can improve your immune system. And the healthier you are, the more random acts you can perform.

There is an endless list of opportunities. Pay attention, get involved, volunteer. Check in with your people, tell them how much you love them, and catch up with one another. I was so surprised when I asked Google for ideas. I read a few that I never even thought of. There is always room to learn something new.

As you already know, I am a grandmother, and my greatest wish is for my grandchildren to grow up in a world where people are considerate and kind. I don't want them to wake up to headlines of shootings and violence. I would love for them to grow up in a loving and kind world. Yes, I have my rose-colored glasses on, but I know in the deepest part of my being that we all have the power to make a difference. One act of kindness at a time!

"The only way to discover the limits of the possible is to go beyond them into the impossible."

~ Arthur C. Clarke

CHAPTER SIX

Self-Reliant Gratitude

By John Spender

Over 20 years ago, I was a door-to-door salesmen walking the suburban streets of Tamworth. The neighborhoods were made up of an eclectic assortment of houses and avenue plantings of trees in between. I had been traversing these streets for two days selling Optus telecommunication lines without a single yes. As the day dragged on, anxiety began to set in as I was on 100% commission and if I didn't make a sale soon, I might not be able to pay my rent. However, at this time in my life, I had begun to study personal development books and seminars. Discouraged by all the rejection I had received in the last 48 hours, I decided it was time for a new plan.

On the third day, I decided that no matter what happened, today was going to be a good day. It didn't matter to me how many people said no or were rude, I was going to remain positive and in good spirits. I would count my blessings as I walked along the footpath, looking for reasons to feel good. I started looking the homeowners directly in their eyes with a big smile on my face as if I already knew them. As the saying goes, when you start feeling appreciative, you get more things to appreciate. Before I knew it, I was on a roll. Almost every door I knocked on opened with a yes. I went from two days without a sale to nineteen sales on the third day. Adopting a happy-go-lucky attitude, appreciating what I had, and detaching from the outcome transformed me from a dedicated sales bum to one of the top performers in one day.

Gratitude is one of the quickest ways I know to turn any situation around as it permeates through everything that you do. People can feel the atmosphere of someone infected with appreciation and positivity. It's one of the easiest things to put into action and it starts with a decision. Deciding to feel good no matter what comes your way. There is always something to be grateful for in your life. Do you have clothes on your back? A roof over your head? Food in the fridge? Can you speak English? Do you have a car to drive to work? Or is public transport available? What about a footpath to walk on? If you answered yes to any of the above questions, you are doing better than most people in the world. If you still find it challenging to find a state of appreciation, I invite you to journal five things a day that you are grateful for in your life.

I recently returned from a trip to Senegal in West Africa. I had a great time and I couldn't help but notice and be grateful for all the things that I take for granted. For example, when I arrived at the airport, I went to use the ATM while I waited for my luggage. You guessed it—the first one didn't work, the second one didn't either, and hoping for the best, I tried the third one, which also didn't work. I had to laugh and feel lucky to live in a country where a working ATM is normal. I wasn't too worried, as I had USD cash, which is accepted everywhere. Lucky enough, when I left the airport, there was one ATM working out of the three machines. Nothing like a travel adventure to remind yourself how blessed your life is and how little others have around the globe.

It doesn't matter where in the world you are; life is a state of consciousness. Whatever you put out will be reflected back to you. The world around you is a reflection of the state of your mindset. Your beliefs will be reflected back to you through your experiences. Who you are is another way of expressing the quantum truth of consciousness. We see reality not as it is but as we are in our beingness. Once you understand this, the relation between consciousness and gratitude or a state of appreciation is easy to see. We elevate our consciousness by seeking the expansion of our appreciation for everything that comes our way. Switching to a "heartset" of kindness towards all life increases through our benevolent deeds—appreciate the good we see, and we will have heaven on Earth. Gratitude consciousness is like a mustard seed that grows and expands until it becomes the greatest of herbs. To expand a balloon, you fill it with air. To expand water, you apply heat. To expand a seed, you bury it in soil. To expand gratitude, you offer appreciation. The consciousness of gratitude is something we must learn to cultivate, nurture, and grow if we are to live a magical life.

Michael Beckwith, one of the greatest spiritual teachers of our time, said, "Gratitude places you in the energy field of plentitude. Perceiving life in a consciousness of gratitude is literally stepping into another dimension of living. Suddenly, the seeming ordinariness of your days takes on a divine sparkle." All of creation responds to appreciation. Animal trainers pet and reward their animals with treats for acts of obedience. Children glow with happiness when they are appreciated. Even vegetation grows better when provided with love and care. When we speak words of encouragement and appreciation to our own abilities, our brain cells augment and increase in capacity and intelligence. Appreciation and gratitude create the same vibration and frequency of positivity and are like inseparable identical twins. Where you find one, you'll find the other. Gratitude is expressing your appreciation, which creates an attitude and environment that is magnetic to other people. Giving thanks heals disease, removes obstacles, and will even open prison doors in the mind. It will do things for us that we can't do for ourselves.

The quickest way to connect and form a communion with the substance of supply, the universal intelligence that governs us all, is through giving appreciation. Stevie Wonder was on to something with his worldwide hit song, "All I Do," with the lyrics:

I thank you baby, bout you baby
I thank you baby, bout you baby
I thank you baby, bout you baby
Give it to me baby, I thank you baby
Yeah, yeah, yeah, yeah, yeah

When a DJ plays this song, you can feel the good vibes increase on the dance floor. I remember I was at a dance festival with friends in Sydney when Dimitri from Paris mixed in "All I Do" by Stevie Wonder, and you should have seen the smiles on everyone's faces. The good vibes were electrifyingly contagious. The crowd moved in appreciation to the funky deco beats. It felt like the collective consciousness of the dance floor was one.

What is the central object of your appreciation from day to day? What is it that you value the most? Is it your family? Well, appreciate them. Is it your wife? Thank her. Whatever you value, make appreciation the foundation and the very presence of your being. Was your breakfast good? Say so; speak it out loud. Did you have a good day at the office? Then, express it. Ride the wave of gratitude. Acknowledge your blessings and watch them multiply.

Looking out the window as I take a break from writing, I stare at a large mango tree, with its green leaves and flowers that will soon turn into fruit. Only a few months earlier, the tree was suffering— probably due to a lack of water, nutrients, and maybe even severed roots from the newly built home. When I saw that tree, I imagined it was healthy with new shoots of green leaves sprouting out all over its canopy. I would send it positive thoughts, appreciating the tree for the shade it provided, the shelter for birds, and the delicious fruits that it was sure to bear. Some may say this is wacky or even kooky. I guess it was a combination of my love for nature and the influence of Dr. David R. Hawkins and his book *Power vs. Force*. In a nutshell, the book is a scientific manifesto of how to use the power we have within our own consciousness as a scale of frequency.

Dr. Hawkins demonstrated through a series of tests in front of live audiences around the world that the subconscious is a living organism that is attuned to recognizing the difference between negative or positive effects on the body. The test required you to place your fingers on someone's arm and push down. When the person is thinking positive thoughts, you won't be able to push their arm down. When the subject thinks negative thoughts, the arm is easily pushed downwards. You begin by pushing their arm down with your fingers. This is easy to test with a friend, and it's a tool that I use in my trainings.

When I began to understand Dr. Hawkins' scale of consciousness and the frequency that different emotional states emit, I started experimenting with that mango tree. I was astounded to see, after a week of sending mental appreciation and praise, the tree began shooting new leaves all over the canopy. A couple of weeks later, my neighbor began watering his garden, as if attuning to my positive vibes. I encourage you to create your own experiment putting gratitude to the test, or at the very least, try Dr. Hawkins' kinesiology process.

Send appreciation to the universe for what you have, and you will receive more of it. Thank her in advance for what you do not have, and those things will be attracted to you through your gratitude. Bless your business, your employees, your customers, and your bank balance. Bless every form of good that you receive. If you want a better job, bless the position you are in. If you are unemployed, bless the perfect position that's waiting for you. By giving thanks, let your request be known to the universe.

Thank the Divine for all the good you wish to receive with an underlying knowingness, and good will be provided in return. Bless your home, your family, your neighbors, your friends, your pets. Let the invisible force of gratitude bless your life. The quickest way to happiness is through the power of appreciation. Give thanks to everything that happens to you, even in crisis, for it is certain that when you express gratitude for it, you transform unfortunate circumstances into blessings that become a valuable lesson and a gift that will serve you for a lifetime.

How will you amplify your consciousness for gratitude except by appreciating all that you have? Review this chapter up until this point and you will see that I have emphasized four main points:

1. The significance of changing your consciousness
2. The significance of keeping gratitude in the forefront of your consciousness
3. The significance of expanding your consciousness
4. The significance of appreciation

This chapter is really a study of gratitude consciousness and developing an understanding of its expansion. Grasping this is of vital importance, as consciousness is the medium through which everything enters or leaves your life. Meditation changes things because it expands your consciousness. It aligns you with your purpose, enabling you to accept and see yourself with an atmosphere of gratitude. Meditation naturally attracts this state of being into your external reality. Consciousness reaches its highest level through the self-forgetfulness that meditation brings to your life. Science has now caught up with what metaphysics has been teaching for years. The science of meditation indicates changes in brain wave frequency expanding one's level of awareness and, in turn, growing your consciousness.

The trouble with most people who find themselves down and unable to feel grateful for anything is the obsession they have with themselves. They do not realize that their lack of gratitude is the very thing that defeats them and keeps them in want, lack, and desperation. What do we say to these people? We shall tell them that the outcome of their difficulty depends entirely on their attitude and habits of mind. If the mind can be kept at least 51%

positive, your attitude will shift into ascending amounts of good vibes and liberation is assured. The attitude or habits of the mind are the determining factors in every problem.

Additionally, in determining how the faculties of the mind will work, one's attitude shapes the speed in which the consciousness will be elevated. Attitude is the cornerstone to raising one's awareness beyond the self. If one's mental level is kept above the 51% positive over negative, the mind will work with the concept of appreciation to open the door to the successful and abundant side of life. If it falls below 50% positive, it will act with failure and lack, accentuating and attracting the difficulties in life.

How shall we increase the mental level into a positive frame of mind? By changing our attitude and expecting the best from every person, place, and thing. We can begin now by assuming our desired virtues through meditation from the circumference to the hub. The circumference represents negative aspects of oneself and the hub is our center, the home of our highest self. The door always opens inwards from our outer reality to our inner reality. A grateful heart can and will develop swiftly once you embrace meditation and all its forms into your daily life.

The first step in expanding your gratitude consciousness is to make meditation the central point of focus. This action will give the mind an upward and forward look, gifting you with a raise in consciousness. This is as simple as meditating every day. The next step is to reverse every negative thought the instant it appears by giving all your power to the consciousness of good. Give no power to failure, delay, doubt, disappointment, despondency, despair, misfortune, or bad luck. Don't get upset when things don't go as expected, and don't expect the worst. Know that your mind has the power to make anything right. You can let go of the negative thoughts and focus on appreciation for the things you have in your life already.

Refuse to remain depressed, disappointed, worried, hesitant, or fearful of uncertainty. When trouble and misfortune come your way, remember that they are only temporary. If you are compelled to raise your degree of consciousness, make sure you are doing some form of meditation, be it traditional meditation, walking in nature, staring at the deep blue ocean, gazing at a fiery sunset, or even quieting your mind as you do the dishes.

Do not let interruptions, recessions, or even global pandemics cause you to lose focus of your highest good. When you meet conflict or disharmony, refuse to become divided or distressed in your thoughts. Remember not to get upset with people or situations; both are powerless without your reaction. Hold rigid to the statement of the Dalai Lama, "When you lose, don't lose the lesson." Look upon defeat, failure, and mistakes as moldable plasticine in your hand. Maintain the attitude and feeling of gratitude that will awaken and bring out the best that's inside of you.

Know that you can change your circumstances and state of affairs by changing your consciousness through the power of meditation. It makes no difference how poorly things may be going in the outer world. Your job is to keep things running smoothly in your own heart and mind. The more you become conscious of your mind, the more your superconscious power will produce results for you. That is the law of attraction. If you train your mind to think in terms of praise, appreciation, and abundance, you will experience an increase in every area of your life. When you give thanks, you continue to receive more things to be thankful for in abundant measure.

Commit now to daily meditation. Begin with five minutes a day, then gradually increase the duration of time. Find a quiet place and sit in comfort. Allow yourself to be still and rest within, focusing on your breath. If you become distracted (and you will!), simply observe the thoughts, then bring your focus back to your breath. Gradually, through repetition and consistency of practice, you will "lose the mind," awakening your senses to the magnificence of your inner world. Slowly but surely, your consciousness will ascend to another level of awareness, embodying higher frequencies and mental states such as gratitude, appreciation, thankfulness, heightened sensitivity, and an energized beingness. In this enlightened state of embodiment, gratitude comes naturally.

"Every condition, every experience in life is a result of our mental attitude. We can do only what we think and feel we can do. We can be only what we think we can be. We can have only what we think we can have. What we do, who we are, and what we have all depend upon what we think and believe is possible. There is only one limit upon the Creative Force, and that is the limit we impose upon it." These were wise words from one of the greatest self-help authors of the 20th century, Robert Collier. All things are possible when we increase our level of consciousness. We can never express anything that we don't have an awareness of in our field of perception. The secret of all power and all success is found through the cognizance of your consciousness. Allow your meditation practice to guide you into an ever-deeper expansion of your consciousness. Watch as your natural attitude evolves towards praise and appreciation for everything in your world.

Eleven Key Principles to Align with Gratitude

Allow the following principles to guide and elevate you to the consciousness highway of goodness, grace, and gratitude:

1. Trust in and surrender to the intelligence that created you. This trust is the foundation for your freedom of expression, which allows you to choose how you feel and not be governed by outside circumstances. When you trust yourself, you are no longer afraid to praise another. Higher consciousness is not just an idea that sounds esoteric and spiritual—it's a beingness. Trust is the gateway to developing your higher self. The more you trust

the wisdom that creates, the more you'll be trusting in yourself. With trust, you enter the higher realms of frequency, vibration, and consciousness, where expressing appreciation is a natural form of being. In order to unlock gratitude, trust is the first key principle that you must come to understand and embrace for the embodiment of the other principles.

2. Develop an inner knowing through a deeper, more profound connection with yourself and the universe at large. This discovery of knowing that you are in everything breeds immeasurable connection and appreciation for all things. Embrace your oneness with the universe and know that you are the universe, and the universe is you. See the beauty in the unfolding of everyday life. Look for the Divine in the seemingly mundane. Allow your intuition to write the script for your life; let it be the guiding light for your masterpiece. Remember, that intuition is your point of connection, with the universe your creator, and your compass for your greater good. This second principle guides us towards a binding alignment with all things encompassing your higher self.

3. Let go of the lies and smile! It's a lie to think that you aren't good enough. It's a lie to think that you don't deserve to be happy. It's a lie to think that you are not worthy. When you catch yourself thinking one of these erroneous thoughts, just smile. Entwine this counterintuitive principle into your consciousness, smile, because in your heart, you know you are blessed. Smiling to correct an error in your thinking is a form of self-praise. When you let go of the lies, you honor and appreciate yourself, which creates space for you to praise others. When you can integrate this principle, you will know gratitude.

4. Acknowledge and appreciate everything that appears in your life, from the Divine to the turbulent, and even the disastrous, for they are leading you towards the greater good in your life. By going within, you will discover that whatever you had experienced bestowed an underlying gift of inner fortitude to overcome

anything in your life, or at least to live in harmony with it. When you can look back with forgiveness and appreciation, even for behavior that doesn't make you proud, you can realize that was who you were at that time. Our behaviors have great lessons attached to them for us to transcend. You will be able to say with certainty, "I am what I am, and the past doesn't reflect my future." While some of the people close to you may find it difficult to accept you, you will no longer compromise yourself. Thanking your past breaks its bondage, creating freedom of choice for this present moment. When you apply this principle, you have made the decision to be free.

5. Align your point of focus. You can't feel praise-worthy and undeserving at the same time. When you catch yourself thinking negative thoughts or about things you don't want, give thanks, and bring your attention back to your desires. The law of focus is in operation regardless of whether you are aware of its existence or not. What you focus on expands, what you focus on seems real, what you focus on, you become. So, when you focus on the good in your life, the good gets better. You begin to generate a momentum of goodness that accentuates your sense of gratitude. Aligning your point of focus and employing this principle for your life affirms what is valuable and necessary for your happiness.

6. Be thankful for your good in advance. Perhaps you are suffering through ill health and the prognosis doesn't look good. Give thanks for the good health that is to come. When you look in the mirror, appreciate yourself as you imagine how good you feel. Doing this is watering the seed of good health that you have planted. In your finances, maybe you are struggling, and business is slow. Affirm with appreciation that whatever you touch prospers and succeeds. Declare your ideal reality throughout the day. When you give thanks in advance, not only does it water the seed, it strengthens your belief and self-esteem. You are appreciating your ideal life and calibrating yourself with the infinite intelligence and

the source of all creation. This principle will support you to move mountains, making the seemingly impossible possible.

7. Adopt the potency of prayer as a heartfelt form of appreciation for all that is and all that ever will be. Prayer is not just a form of asking, it's also a form of giving thanks to your higher self. It's a way to acknowledge yourself and connect deeper within beyond the surface reality of day-to-day living. Develop a sacredness that guides you through prayer. Allow prayer to cultivate the good and rid yourself of ego-dominating thoughts so you can grow your connection to Divinity. Heaven on Earth is a choice that we decide to make, not a place we must find.

"Dear Universe/God, I appreciate you for granting me the inner peace, wisdom, and stability to inspire heaven in my home and community. I thank you for all that I have and all that I am. I appreciate your light that steers me to grow and evolve into the best version of myself, in good health and percipience. And so, it is."

Your dedication to this principle of prayer will open opportunities in your life that you never knew existed.

8. Acknowledge and appreciate the challenges of your lineage. Your ancestors endured struggles and difficulties that paved the way for a better life for you. Maybe they had to cross oceans with the threat of pirates or endure a world war. Be thankful for the struggles and adversity that they undoubtedly conquered just so you can live your life today. Consider visiting the gravesite of your ancestors and acknowledge their existence with your presence, appreciating their lives. Even visiting your local cemetery and expressing gratitude for the lives of another human being's journey will breed the attitude of appreciation within your consciousness. This principle of remembering the evolution of life calls for us to remember those who laid the path for us to walk on.

9. Wake up to the gift of breath. Becoming conscious of your breath is to bring your beingness into present-moment awareness

of the here and now, the domain of infinite possibilities. Open up to its tranquil guidance like the touch of the first rays of sunlight of a cool spring morning. Surrender to its softness and unwavering support. Nothing is possible without the breath, yet it is so easy to take it for granted. We can last a month or even longer without food. Without water, we will perish within three to four days. However, the cells in the brain will begin dying within three minutes without oxygen. Spiritual teacher Cristen Rodgers said, "Each breath is like a little rebirth, a renaissance that can only be celebrated if we recognise that it's happening." This principle is urging us to heighten our relationship with the breath and recognize its presence with your appreciation.

10. Demonstrate your appreciation and praise for your body temple and the environment at large. When we make venerable choices for our bodies, we align ourselves with the greater good of all. If we can appreciate ourselves, we can thank our planet by adjusting the way we treat it. We have a symbiotic relationship with our environment; what affects one effects the other. A perfect example of this is the sea anemone and the clownfish. They coexist in harmony, each providing a benefit for the other. The anemone provides shelter and protection for the clownfish. In return, the clownfish cleans the anemone of parasites. Their relationship is one of appreciation. This principle brings us to a place of honoring our symbiotic relationship with the Earth through appreciating our own existence.

11. Declare your gratitude and appreciation through affirmations. Our brains are not naturally wired for gratitude. Survival is the chief aim of the mind, and without heedful awareness, the mind can automatically run things. To avoid fearful living, repeat positive affirmations to remind and program your mind, expanding your consciousness and heartfelt gratefulness. Meditating before you affirm anything quiets the mind, shifting the brain from a beta-wave frequency to an alpha state. It's a mistake to say your affirmations while not in a positive frame of mind. It's the easiest

thing in the world to get caught up with distractions, negativity, and other people's drama and forget about your own dreams and desires. Make this conditioning principle part of your daily ritual meditation to affirm the reality you want to live.

Here are 11 positive affirmations to begin your practice:

* I appreciate all that I am and all that I have.
* I give generously to myself.
* I know what I love to do, and I do it.
* I love and accept myself just the way I am.
* Every gift I give serves and empowers others.
* I send love to my fears, which are places within me that await my love.
* Every gift I give is a gift for myself. As I give, I receive.
* As I live in present moment awareness, I live the magic of synchronicity.
* I appreciate myself. I give thanks for my awesome life.
* The things that I create are even better than I imagined them to be.
* I am what I am, and what I am is a spark of God force, and that God force is all compassion and forgiveness.

As you embody the above principles, notice how you can evoke overwhelming states of appreciation and practically lose the ability to worry. As you awaken to gratitude consciousness, accepting your life for all it is and isn't, you'll begin to have frequent, overwhelming episodes of gratitude. Everything becomes a miracle. You become aware of how much you have to be thankful for, and there is no room for scantiness or meagerness, as it is no longer your point of focus.

As the embodiment of being your own miracle takes hold, a heightened awareness of gratitude transforms life from a competitive arena into a realm of shared enrichment where collaboration thrives, ensuring victory for all. Perhaps your journey mirrors mine—engaging in door-to-door sales, wrestling with discouragement fueled by rejections, and witnessing negativity cloud your perspective. Yet, remember, in moments of defeat, the power to swiftly shift your consciousness from scarcity to gratitude lies within your grasp. By living in a perpetual state of gratitude, you inflate like a balloon, expanding until you burst through to the radiant heights of an appreciation-driven consciousness, becoming a beacon of your own miraculous transformation.

**"Miracles happen every day.
Not just in remote country villages
or holy shrines halfway across the
globe, but right where you are,
in your own life."**

~ Unknown

CHAPTER SEVEN

———◦○◦———

Healthy Choices

By Annette Forsythe

"Hi! How are you?"

Do you use that greeting regularly? And if you do pose that innocent inquiry into another's well-being, do you listen for a real answer, or do you automatically hear the socially acceptable "Fine," and move on?

Since John and I began to outline this book, I have stressed over this chapter. Not for lack of subject matter, but because of the self-deprecating patterns that live in my head. Where does someone who looks like me come off speaking about health? I don't exactly resemble the picture of health most people would carry around in their heads.

Yet health is not just your physical state of being or a list of medical diagnoses. Health is the state of your mind, body, and spirit, or more formally, your mental, physical, and emotional state. The combination of these three aspects of health fuels the stories I have to share on this subject.

More often than not, we live our lives according to a series of reflexive beliefs and behaviors—patterns. We are not born with these patterns, but we do inherit them as we grow from infancy. They are already there for us in our surroundings with our families. First, we learn our behaviors, and these behaviors shape our worldview. So, by the time we're ready to think on our own, we are pretty set on the way we will see things. The patterns are entrenched. These patterns tell us how to act, respond, or think about everything. Then, we begin putting our spin on these patterns based on our own experiences. Next, we have significant emotional events. These events are life changing and leave lasting effects that either feed the existing patterns or make new ones. Patterns do a great job showing us the way; they give us a way of navigating an unfamiliar and frightening world as we grow. There's only one problem: even though they serve and protect, patterns do not always act in our own best interest.

The good news is that we are not our patterns. We can get rid of the old and build new ones that better help us.

Let me explain by example. I was raised in a very old-fashioned Italian family. Life happened around the dining room table, and the answer to everything was food. Whether happy, sad, or grief-stricken—just eat, you'll feel better. Not surprisingly, I grew up a chubby kid, teenager, and adult. Food was always my safety net, but I paid a price for the comfort it provided. Over those years, many significant events only strengthened my belief that I wasn't good enough because of how I looked.

First came the "If only . . ." statementsYour face is so beautiful. If only you could lose ten pounds," was often commented. "You look so lovely. If only you could lose ten pounds, another person would chime in." Gradually, this spread to other parts of my life; anything I had done could be great, "if only," and it went on and on. As time passed, "if only" combined with the verbal hits of "You're an embarrassment;" "You'll never be in the same class of people;" "You're too ugly to love;" "Your husband will never be faithful;" and "She's wider than he is tall," to quote just a few. These jabs created a strong belief that I would never be worthy or good enough. I never felt like I belonged, and as a result, I tried to blend into the background and not be seen. This pattern had a hold on me and led me to take comfort in the very thing that had brought me down. I would eat for comfort—a roller coaster of emotions that has haunted me my entire life. Every accomplishment I made and every challenge I took on took a backseat. Nothing I did was considered enough because I did not look like I was someone who deserved success.

This kind of story is not uncommon. So many people in the world are walking around feeling they are not good enough. The healing happens when you finally address this feeling.

I carried this burden for years. The patterns of a lifetime gave me everything I needed to stay stuck in a very unhealthy place. Finally, I realized I had to take responsibility for my behavior. Deep in my heart, I knew all those comments came from places of love or ignorance, and yet, I still chose to self-destruct.

Then came the tricky part. Having accepted where my hurt came from, now my actions needed to reflect that acceptance. The comments were forgiven years ago. I was the one replaying them in my head, keeping the unhealthy patterns alive and well, giving them the power to downplay anything I've accomplished. I had to take responsibility and own my choices. How would I respond and replace these patterns?

Old habits die hard. I had to learn to "see" myself, not the outer shell, but the inside. I had to stop attaching my self-worth to my physical body.

All the revelations and the emotions that tagged along impacted my health in the worst possible way. Stress, fatigue, and depression kept my state of being and my energy very low. That low energy made every task harder to do.

Dr. John Sarno has written several books about pain and the mind/body connection. I could easily be his poster child. When my stress level is up, my pain levels follow right along.

At first, I was annoyed when this was pointed out to me by my business partner. Really? Who wants to be a stereotype? But my business partner was right. Insidious onsets of pain are usually connected to stressful things happening in my life—the mind-body connection! It's like a miracle. If you deal with the problem, then the pain goes away. Sounds easy enough, but the dealing part takes work, and you have to be willing to do it.

In my experience, when people have been through challenging events, a physical breakdown usually follows. I am convinced the stress of these situations can cause serious health issues.

We have all just lived through a terrible crisis called COVID-19. This pandemic has taken a toll on all of us, especially mentally. Months in isolation, fear of this "invisible" virus that was out there to get us. So much information overload on the news. All the loss and being separated from our loved ones. Even after all this time, I still have anxiety when I think about it.

Personally, the only way I could get through these last couple of years was to adapt to a new mindset. As hard as it was to accept, I had absolutely no control over all the craziness. The only thing I could control was how I showed up.

Learning to accept that saved me. I was able to let go of so much angst. It put me in a calm state and kept me from the downward spiral that could have taken hold otherwise, allowing me to face the other challenges that lay ahead and keep my blood pressure under control. To maintain our health, our mind, body, and spirit must be intact. We can't function properly if we are not taking care of ourselves. Self-care is a must; proper nutrition for fuel, exercise for energy, and sound sleep to regenerate.

On an airplane, the safety video tells you to put your own oxygen mask on first, and then you can help others. We have to keep our health a priority.

To give you an example from my own life, this summer was an eye-opening experience for me. Over this time, I have found a whole new meaning to the importance of healthy choices: a family heartache and a family crisis both on the same day. There was nothing I could do but accept the heartache as something I had no control over, but I could certainly show up to support the crisis.

Good news never comes late at night. My phone rang after I had gone to bed. It was my sister. My brother-in-law had fallen and had been taken to a trauma center in Asheville, NC. He had broken six ribs and had a collapsed lung and fluid in his chest. There were two emergency surgeries in one day. His movements after the first surgery caused one of the broken ribs to puncture his diaphragm, and he was taken back to the operating room. They didn't know if he would survive.

I got on a plane as soon as possible to be there for both of them. I went into protective mode: protect my sister, support her through this nightmare, and make sure she ate and slept—that was my job. I wasn't allowed in the hospital, so I would drop my sister off in the morning and sit in the parking lot so that I could be near her. Then, when she needed a break, I would have coffee and a snack waiting. There was a medical team taking care of my brother-in-law. My sister needed me to hold her up.

The hospital was an hour from their home, so we stayed at a hotel. It only took a few days before we had our routine together. I stayed by her side until my brother-in-law was sent to rehab. We believed things were going uphill, and so I returned home.

The day after I returned, I was physically and emotionally exhausted, but I had no time to recover, as I urgently needed to move locations with my physical therapy business. Completely distracted, I tripped on the carpet, fell, and hit the corner of a chair and bumped my head on the table. It wasn't pretty and required a trip to the emergency room. I had broken a rib and hurt my foot. But I would deal with it. I had things to do. I had to support my sister and I had a business to move.

Returning to work was almost a reprieve. It was something to do every day, even if it did hurt to breathe. Business as usual and more preparations for the move.

The normalcy didn't last long. After my brother-in-law was discharged from rehab, he unexpectedly passed away. My sister was completely distraught. A week later, it was back to North Carolina, and my mama bear instincts were running high!

I did a good job ignoring my broken rib and paid no attention as my foot got worse for wear. I had things to do. Those three weeks in North Carolina passed in a blur. Finally, once I was back home, the foot needed my attention. Imagine my surprise when I found out I had been walking on a fractured ankle for three weeks! I guess that explained my foot pain. And it was only a few weeks from moving day.

I think I carried my sister's grief as well as my own. All I know is I felt torn in half. My heart needed to be with my sister, and my business needed to move and grow. So, I just went into automatic pilot mode and did my best to be there for her and the business.

Stress levels were at new highs. Heartache, grief, stress, broken bones, and my rheumatoid arthritis did not play nice together. I was crippled emotionally and physically, yet I kept pushing through. I was set in the pattern of being strong for my sister, so I told myself I would keep being strong no matter the cost. I had to protect the things and people I loved.

And so it went on for months, until, finally, I was spiraling—and I didn't care. I just didn't care. I didn't have the energy. In fact, I didn't have the energy for anything. I got so sick, I was bedridden for a week. I felt completely broken. This was the extreme wake-up call that made me realize I couldn't keep going like I was. I needed to care for myself because my life depended on it!

Through all these events, I had been ignoring all the things I preach about. I wasn't sleeping. I didn't eat properly. I stopped moving. I forgot about my health and well-being. And now I had collapsed, and I was no use to anyone. This is why they tell you to put your oxygen mask on first before helping anyone else.

It has taken time, but I have begun piecing my health back together with lots of support and guidance from chosen family members. I try to take things one day at a time. I have set myself on a journey to create a new identity where I actually love myself and choose to follow all the tools I have learned through the years.

I had to appreciate there was a lesson to be learned in everything that had happened. I began by defining what I had control over. I could control my reactions. I could control how I fueled and hydrated my body, own my state of mind, and manage my choices to be active. I would work to create good habits and let the habits get the results.

I reached out for accountability and guidance, and my supporters have been there for me every step of the way. I have had a few bouts of emotional behavior, but I can recognize them and stop the pattern. Half the battle is awareness. Movement has been a little more challenging because of my RA. Baby steps and short intervals are essential right now. As for my mental health, meditation has had a significant impact. I keep myself grounded and visualize happier, healthier days.

These past months have taught me so much. As the old saying goes, you don't know what you have until it's gone. Good health is not to be taken for granted and taking care of ourselves is non-negotiable. Even with the best intentions, sometimes the choices we make do more harm than good. Someone once told me, "Nothing tastes as good as healthy feels."

Recently, I was part of a conversation in my "growth" community. My friend and mentor, Rod Hairston, posed this question: "How do you envision your quality time remaining?" Considering I have a "big" birthday (that would be 65) looming in front of me, that question had a significant impact on me.

After a lifetime of self-doubt, I owe it to myself to ensure I make the best choices for myself. I refuse to spend one more minute selling myself short. I have been married for forty-one years, raised four incredible women, volunteered in my community, and ran a business for twenty-two years. These are magnificent accomplishments, no matter what I look like. My "QTR" is going to be filled with adventure and joy.

If we don't meet our own needs first, we cannot accomplish anything—not for us, not for others. We cannot live to our full potential without our health, and good health begins with healthy choices for our welfare.

"You are not here merely to make a living. You are here in order to enable the world to live more amply, with greater vision, with a finer spirit of hope and achievement."

~ Woodrow Wilson

CHAPTER EIGHT

---∘◦✑✑◦∘---

Tools For Change: Laying the Foundation for Self-Reliance

By John Spender

I didn't always have a successful, productive business. I had many years of struggle being ruled by my emotions, not knowing where to start. I rarely stuck to my commitments and I wondered why I had low self-esteem. Have you ever felt like you needed fixing, going from one seminar to another, riding one endless loop but never really feeling like you are getting somewhere? When I started deleting all my excuses and taking responsibility for my life through action, my confidence grew along with my self-belief. With this mindset, we can move mountains. My life became a series of priorities that enhanced my life, that life works for us, not against, and everything is happening for our greater good. I discovered what I loved to do and I made time for these activities and naturally found my inner happiness. Something magical happens when we view miracles as a form of change. I invite you to take notes and to experience everyday miracles as you walk the courageous path into the unknown.

Principle 1: Get a Mentor

"If you always do what you've always done, you'll always get what you got." That's a great quote by Tony Robbins that rings true for just about all of us. For those who haven't heard of Tony, he is the most famous face in the personal development industry. He runs seminars all over the world, including on his resort island in

Fiji. Tony has also coached the likes of Andre Agassi, Bill Clinton, and multi-billionaires. I love that quote and it's had a significant impact on so many people's lives, including my own. It's vital that any time we desire to create and attract a miracle, we need to be different. That's why it's handy to have a mentor who is already living in the place we desire. You can have Tony Robbins as your mentor simply by consuming his books and his content that is readily available on YouTube, as well as his numerous online seminars. All it takes is a commitment to show up and do the work. I've been to many of his conferences, read his books, and watched him on YouTube. I feel he's just an awesome person to have influenced your life.

The late Dr. Wayne Dyer has been another person who has been a great mentor of mine. He was a metaphysical professor at Wayne State University before starting a counseling practice in New York. His breakthrough moment was launching the book *Your Erroneous Zones* in 1976 and was coined the "Father of Motivation." He has spoken to thousands of people on stages around the world, having released more than 30 personal development and higher consciousness books. I've been to his workshops and read his books, and he helped me change the way I viewed being kind to other people. He inspired me to volunteer at Mission Australia in Sydney, assisting the borderline homeless with change workshops every Tuesday using neuro-linguistic programming. It was such a beautiful shift in my life. I'm forever grateful for his presence.

When we want to make a change, we need to step outside of our comfort zone. So, studying with someone who has already made the change you aspire to make is a huge advantage and it makes the transition much easier. Let's face it, if we're not growing, we're dying; this is the whole evolution of the universe. We are meant to grow; we are meant to challenge ourselves; we are built for adversity to expand, grow, and become a greater version of ourselves.

One of Dr. Dyer's favorite sayings was, "Don't die with your music still inside you," and it's so true. I was in a cemetery in Los Angeles and it left me wondering how many people had gone to their graves with their music unexpressed, gifts inside, dreams unfulfilled. You know what's worse than dying? Dying with your potential not acknowledged, without pursuing your dream; even if you fail, at least you gave it a shot. Anytime I find myself caught between making a change or not, where I'm like 50-50, should I or should I not, I do the rocking chair test. The rocking chair test is this: when I'm 90 years old, sitting in my rocking chair on my front porch, would I regret not making that change? Would I regret not pursuing that opportunity? Would I regret not taking a risk, whatever it may be? It's an easy way to decide if I should step into the unknown.

The hard part is facing the truth; the right choice is most often the most challenging path, and the correct answer can bring up a lot of emotions and fears. It usually means stepping up to be a bigger person and playing a bigger game in life. We can get caught up with wanting to know the outcome and wanting reassurance that everything will go according to plan. When we see that we are entertaining the HOW, the how of "Is this going to work?" the how can also bring up fears like, "Am I worthy? Am I good enough? Am I afraid of success?" None of that is true. It's just the process of being stuck in the HOW.

A better alternative is to trust your truth and get excited about not knowing the outcome. I know what people say: you need to plan, and if you don't plan, you plan to fail. I prefer to start with the desired outcome I'm looking for in any situation. For all you die-hard planners, let me ask you a question. How many plans have you developed in great detail which have gone according to that plan? The answer for me is not once! And I know what you die-hard planners are saying: "What about the contingency plan?" Let it go already. With all that time you spent planning, you could have completed the task. It's all about the result, baby, and getting there any way you can!

When you know you need to make a change, you have a choice; it's like taking off a Band-Aid. You can either take it off slowly or rip it off quickly. The decision's yours. Find your vision, refine it, and let the universe take care of the how. Your alignment to your vision attracts what you need at the right time. It's the magnetism for miracles.

Principle 2: Set Clear Intentions

Intention deficit disorder—what does it mean exactly?! I recently caught up with Reverend Michael Beckwith for a film I'm producing about discovering the gift in adversity. I interviewed him for about 40 minutes. If you haven't heard of him, he starred in the hit documentary *The Secret*, he is the founder of the spiritual center Agape in Los Angeles, California, and he is just an all-around inspiring guy.

One of the many things he said that resonated with me was his insight into people and humanity. He said that people suffer from "intention deficit disorder." Many people have no apparent intention for what they would like to change in their lives. Intention deficit disorder is a form of resistance to change, the passive kind. It's when you don't set an intention for your day, week, and life. It's not having a clear intention of what you want to do in life. You know, what's your intention with having an intimate relationship, your intention with your career, your intention with your passion, and your intention with things that you enjoy doing that make you feel alive? The more I set intentions for different aspects of my life, the less dramatic and unsettling the changes I experience are. When you set intentions, your resistance to change isn't as great, and your focus and purpose for the bigger picture of your life can unfold naturally.

A perfect example would be: I set an intention one morning to start a new fitness regime with the desire to get super fit. In Bali, where I lived for nine years, a local Freelectics group met twice a week. I intended to make it through the set; they have a bunch of exercises where they do a lot of jumping jacks, lunges, and various intense exercises that get the heart pumping. My intention was just to finish, make it through, and complete all the activities. I'm usually the last to finish and most of the group finishes early and doesn't complete the workout; it's literally go hard or go home, and most of the group goes home early. I just finished the two sets of exercises that I needed to do, because that was my intention. It was a deliberate intention that I set before I got out of bed. When you set clear intentions and follow through with them, you increase your confidence and self-esteem, and this draws miracles to you, like iron to a magnet.

Making the change from unfit to fit takes discipline, and the deliberate action of setting an intention makes it much more manageable. Initially, it can be challenging, but then you fall into a routine and it becomes easier. Have a single-minded focus and have that intention for the day, and it's amazing to see how it actually plays out as the day unfolds.

The synchronicity that I've had with this film project has been incredible. I woke up one Sunday around the end of December 2015 and I felt an overwhelming sense of fear and doubt. I started talking to my fear out loud, saying that "I need someone with film experience to give me more in-depth feedback on what I should do next." I had just filmed a bunch of guests, but I felt like I was still finding my direction with the storyline. So off I went to play indoor cricket and completely forgot about my conversation with my fear and doubt. We lost the cricket match in a close game. During the game, I was introduced to this American guy watching his first cricket game. We had a brief chat and that was it.

Most of the guys go to the local Aussie pub after every match and I usually go straight home as I rarely drink alcohol. However, on this occasion, my intuition decided that I should go. When I arrived at the pub, I walked straight to the bar and ordered a fresh papaya juice, and the American guy, Adam, was standing at the bar. He also wasn't drinking alcohol and was just standing by himself. We naturally started chatting and it turned out that he was a movie/documentary producer. Boom! We talked for a good hour and he told me about his current film project with all the different challenges they were facing and how they were overcoming them. He became an advisor for my documentary and I have come along leaps and bounds with the project. I'm now talking to an award-winning director about filming the drama scenes.

For me, that's a perfect example of being willing to meet your miracles and do something that you wouldn't normally do on many levels. When you incite change, even if it's scary at first, you are making changes by choice, not changes that surprise you. Talk to your fears. Don't just listen to them and obey their commands. Have a rational conversation with your fears and ask them to bring you your ideal outcome, now that you have intended to forget about it and expect miracles to happen.

Principle 3: Stick to Your Commitments

Managing negative mind chatter can be tricky and frustrating at times, especially when you're walking toward the unknown or doing something for the first time. When I created the first A Journey of Riches book, I went through periods of self-doubt so many times. I soon discovered the importance of saying daily affirmations, doing daily exercise, meditating daily, and talking to friends who had written books and launched bestsellers. My friends weren't going to do the work for me, but it certainly helped to hear their words of wisdom. Having daily routines that keep you healthy and happy is essential to controlling the negative mind chatter rather than letting it direct you. Now, this isn't new information, and almost everyone knows it, but it's a whole other story putting it into action.

Taking action can, at times, be a gap that is too big to leap across and maintain the consistency required to achieve your desired outcome. When your desire is strong enough, the drive and motivation flow naturally, making it easier to keep your mind, body, and spirit sharp. The enjoyment of your routines is another key factor in sticking with them. When it comes to affirmations, I keep them very simple. Some of my favorites are:

- I send love to my fears. My fears are places within me that await my love.

- I love the highest and best in all people. So, I now draw the highest and best people to me.

- I'm always in the right place at the right time to attract magical experiences.

- I radiate self-esteem, inner love, well-being, and happiness.

- I appreciate all that I have and all that I desire.

Every morning, I say around 50 different affirmations while I'm in a meditative state for at least 11 minutes. As a result, your belief begins to soar and your confidence grows, and the action steps become easier to take.

Showing up is one of the most critical steps, because there is no chance of getting a result if you don't at least show up. But sometimes, we don't feel like showing up and taking action. You have to do the task at hand first and then the feeling of satisfaction comes afterward. I don't always feel like doing certain aspects of collating a book, but when I take action despite my mood, the feeling of enjoyment finds me quickly and even more so when I start to make progress.

I can't emphasize enough the importance of simply showing up. Just doing small easy action steps to start with is a great approach.

I learned this from Robert Kayasaki; just keep turning up and underachieving. That's right. Underachieving. I know this sounds counterintuitive, so let me explain. First, you want to establish a new habit. Say you want to get fit and go to the gym. When you're at the gym, you might do one exercise—say, go on the bike for 15 minutes—and then go home.

This is easy and leaves you wanting more. It leaves you thinking, "Why can't I do more? I can do more." When I get writer's block, I will just write 300 words and that's it. It doesn't even have to make sense, but this small action creates momentum. Soon enough, my writing begins to flow. It's creating a game where winning is easy and you're in the zone before you know it.

I also know that sometimes we need to take extended breaks and a breather from our commitments before we start new ones. Sometimes we need to chill, relax, and re-charge our batteries. I was recently able to combine my commitments and include time to recharge. I went to the U.S. to work on the current film I'm producing, where we were interviewing and filming Jack Canfield, Casey Plouffe, and Jessica Cox. I went for a month, had time off between shots, and did some sightseeing and relaxation. This enabled me to be fresh and alert in all my interviews for the film. Recharging the batteries is a gift that we all deserve to give ourselves, and at times, it becomes necessary to rekindle our connection with life. It allows me to come back to whatever I'm doing bigger, better, and more aligned with my purpose, with increased focus.

Principle 4: You Don't Need Fixing

You don't need fixing because you're not broken. You are perfect just the way you are! I know, I hear it; but this, but that, but I got angry last week. Everything is playing out as a divine higher purpose. Everything is a gift if you are open enough to see it. If we open our hearts enough to see it, every action has an advantage. No more beating yourself up, no more berating yourself, no more "but ifs," no more perfection. Isn't it true that we find perfection when we embrace what "is," we accept what "is," and we accept perfection in imperfection? Nature does this perfectly.

I was recently in Singapore, where I spent an hour or so in nature. It was simply beautiful. Just the connection to the wildlife and the plants, birds came straight up to me, and fish swam to me. I wasn't thinking, "If only I did this," "If I only had that," or "This is missing from my life." I wasn't focusing on outside circumstances. I was just being present in the moment and allowing nature to come to me. It was so peaceful, so serene. Knowing we are the thinker of our thoughts and the feeler of our emotions empowers us to see that we are alright as we are.

Self-sabotaging behaviors and that little voice sometimes seem incessant and won't shut up! We need to be our own best friends. Back in early 2000, in one of her audios, Louise Hay said, "Be still with yourself and be your own best friend." Be kind to yourself, speak words of encouragement, and praise yourself. When you start to do this, it is much easier for you to compliment and be encouraging to other people. Then, things begin to shift and change. You begin to like your soul, but you begin to appreciate others more. Generally, if a person has no friends, they don't like themselves. They don't want anyone. See your greatness, see your beauty, recognize your awesomeness, start seeing it in other people, and awaken it within yourself.

Principle 5: Believe in Yourself

What I've found made a difference when I was transitioning from my landscaping business into coaching, speaking, writing, and now making my first movie was actually helping other people that didn't believe in themselves. There are so many people out in the world who have self-esteem much lower than yours. So, helping them helps you as you are going through your transition or significant change, especially if it is something to do with your career, which was my case.

I volunteered my time at Mission Australia in Sydney, helping people who were borderline homeless and were just hard out on their luck. Many of them suffered addiction or needed extreme medications to help them maintain stability. When I went there, I was learning NLP (neuro-linguistic programming) at the time and I had just finished my practitioner's training certificate. I shared with the group what I knew. At that stage, I had never done any public speaking before and I thought I was going to die; really, it was super scary. But you know what? I got in front of those people and was super surprised at the difference I was making. My self-belief went through the roof; it was sky-high after that and it wasn't too long after this experience that I received my first paying coaching client.

What I recommend to people is to help those who have less belief in themselves than you do. If they have low self-esteem, lower confidence, or are more fearful, help them and you'll witness your miracle. Your enthusiasm, self-belief, and self-esteem will soar as a result. I strongly recommend to my coaching clients that when they want to raise their self-esteem, they seek out people or a situation to support or volunteer their time to a not-for-profit organization. Plus, they should do one thing every day that brings happiness and joy to their life.

Another thing that I liked to do when I lived in Bali was volunteer my time at the Hope Children's Home orphanage. That was a fantastic experience. There are a lot of kids there that are very sad. On the outside, they can be pleased, but when you talk to them and dig a little deeper, there's a lot of disappointment left unexpressed—being around kids and people less fortunate than yourself can make a huge difference to their life, as well as your own. When we help other people believe in themselves, some of that magic rubs off onto us.

Principle 6: Cure Yourself of Excusitis

What is excusitis and how can you overcome it? How often have you gone to do something and you haven't followed through, you just found an excuse instead? For example, you decided that you were going to go jogging four days a week, and you're good for the first week, then the second week you miss two days, and then you find it's almost impossible to go jogging early in the mornings again. The excuses that come up are endless; you forgot to set the alarm, you just didn't feel like it, you ate way too much at dinner the night before, whatever it may be. It's one of the largest forms of resistance to building self-reliance in one's life.

This word has been taken from the famous book, *The Magic of Thinking Big* by David Schwartz—Chapter Two: Cure Yourself of Excusitis, the Failure Disease. He uses the word "Excusitis" (from the root word "excuse"), which he defined as "The disease of the failures." He said, "Every failure has this disease in its advanced form." And yes, it's contagious. So, if your close friends are always making excuses, you will eventually do the same.

One of the things that I work on with some of my clients is how to overcome excusitis and become aligned with their values, dreams, and desires. First, you need to take away all the excuses. It would help if you made it easy to avoid the reasons in the first place and form a new habit and goal.

First, you need to have an accountability partner, someone who will hold you accountable. This can be as simple as checking in each week, having a weekly review to see what's happening and if you're being true to your commitment. The chances of you letting yourself down by not making the new habit are pretty high, actually, but the chances of you letting someone else and yourself down are lower. Therefore, your chances of success increase. Most people don't want to let a good friend down.

The second thing is to develop a more significant reason for forming the new habit. What is the purpose of creating the new routine? For example, going jogging a few times a week could be a new habit. This could be because you're over the fact that when you are playing with the kids in the park, you're puffed after ten minutes, you're exhausted and can't continue, and you feel embarrassed. This means you're missing connection time with your children. That's a pretty strong purpose, a strong motivator, and a reason to go running in the mornings and get fit. The secret is you need to attach it to something meaningful to you that's worth doing.

Thirdly, you want to make a public declaration. Declare to as many people as possible that you will set a new habit, a new routine. You need to communicate what this is and what you are going to do because then you won't want to look silly in front of many people. That's why you need to declare your intention. I've done this on Facebook and when I was taking part in a speaker and trainers program back in late 2010 in Sydney.

The program went over five days and the second-to-last night was called outrageous night. This is where the 180 participants got dressed up in outrageous costumes and then had to sing a 2-minute song of their choice on stage. We were divided into two groups of around ninety people each and the instruction was to express yourself in any way that would be a challenge for you. How it worked was the MC would call someone to the stage and then there would be another three people lined up next to the stage, ready to sing their song.

I wanted to be the best speaker that I could develop into and give myself the ultimate challenge. When they called my name out to line up, everyone started to cheer, but this quickly faded as everyone was in fancy dress except me. People were disappointed at my lack of effort. As I stood in line, I began to take off my shoes, socks, and T-shirt. As I moved second in line, I took off my jeans and a few people started to notice. I saw them pointing at me and talking to each other. Even before that, I was having heart palpitations and it felt like I was going to die. I started counting four seconds on my in-breath, holding for four seconds, breathing out for four seconds, and holding my breath for another four seconds.

This breathing technique was my savior. It was now my turn to stand first in line, ready to go on stage. Remember, I was standing there in my underwear. As the MC called my name to go on stage, I whipped off my underwear and walked onto the stage in my birthday suit!

The loud gasp from the 90-odd people in the audience rang through my ears as I stood on stage completely naked.

Before each person could sing their song and act outrageously, you had to stand on stage with your arms wide open, completely exposed, to receive an energy whoosh. This is when the audience claps their hands together three times and, after the third clap, projects their energy and arms out towards you while making a whoosh sound.

My adrenaline began to kick in and I don't remember feeling the energy whoosh. Still, I remember feeling significantly supported and the looks of disbelief, encouragement, and excitement will stay with me forever. I also remember not wanting to look down as the air conditioning made the room very cold, like very cold. Time was in slow motion until I started singing "Relax, Don't Do It," by Frankie Goes to Hollywood, and I was jumping all over the stage singing the chorus repeatedly. That didn't matter as the crowd was going crazy, banging on the stage, wolf-whistling, and cheering with excitement.

Before I knew it, the music stopped but the cheering and excitement kept ringing in my ears. With my heart pumping fast and filled with excitement, shame, and euphoria all rolled into one. Again, I had to stand with my arms wide open and receive an energy woosh. I had never been so exposed in my whole life and so accepted in my entire life. It was overwhelming. During the break, I had several women I had never met before who wanted to hug and kiss me.

It was such a surreal experience, and I don't think I would have done it if I didn't tell my friends in my group what I was going to. I told at least five of them and tried to encourage them to do it too, but they were like, "No way!" There was no chance I could back out. The pain of them teasing me or seeing me as a person who was all talk and no action was greater than me challenging myself and going on stage naked. So now, when I'm on stage at different venues worldwide, I speak with my clothes on!

The fourth thing you want to have is a reward for following through. It could be that you get to go out on a date night with your wife to your favorite restaurant. Whatever it may be, the reward needs to feel good. I treated myself to all-I-could-eat sushi after my nude singing performance.

The fifth step is you need to have a consequence—that's right! a consequence for not following through. It could be your neighbor gets to put a cream pie in your face, or it could be that you'll donate to a particular political party, a political party that you just hate and it would be an absolute nightmare for you to have to shell out some coin from your wallet to this political party that you can't stand. The thought of the consequence should just disgust you so that it is a strong incentive to keep your word.

To recap on how to overcome excusitis and make any change in your life:

1. Have an accountability partner
2. Declare to many people and even post your intention on social media

3. Have a strong reason/purpose driving you forward
4. Reward; the greater the risk, the greater the reward
5. Have a deterrent/consequence; a strong motivator

So there you have it, my fundamentals for overcoming excusitis and magnetizing the miracles in your life.

Principle 7: Priority Management

"I'm too busy." I hear that all the time. People tell me, "I've just been so busy with the different projects that I'm working on and deadlines." It comes down to priority management, prioritizing your schedule, prioritizing the things that you need to get done because, let's face it, everyone's busy. Even my mum, who's retired, is busy. If you become sick, you would go to the doctor. You wouldn't say, "I'm too busy to go to the doctor . . ." No, you make it a priority to go to the doctor. It's not time management that's needed when building resilience and walking through the unknown, it's priority management. It's impossible to manage time. You can only control what you do within the time you are given. Change can seem effortless when you've got your priorities right and you hardly notice it.

When dealing with change or challenging circumstances, priority management is your best friend. I list the top five things that I want to get done for the day and then get them out of the way. This creates momentum and takes care of the busy feelings.

Busyness comes down to fear. It's an excuse, and what you are saying is the task wasn't a high enough priority, or maybe you felt too afraid to tackle it. You didn't feel worthy enough to go for it. So, for tomorrow or this week, I challenge you to prioritize your day, list the highest-priority tasks, and get them out of the way first.

When we are in a state of fear, it's easy to get busy, it's easy to check social media, it's easy to get distracted, and distraction stops us from facing the task at hand. There's often a fear associated with doing the task and fears can be embedded deep into the subconscious mind. That's why we avoid doing it. Filling your day with meaningless activities is a symptom of fearing change. Change isn't the problem. It's the fear of change, the unknown, and wanting to stay safe. Becoming organized and prioritizing our day can help bring our fears to the surface so we can face the fear, process it, and move on.

Principle 8: Tap Into Your Inner Happy

Happiness and laughter are two of the best tools to build resilience and walk toward your miracles. One of the most accessible forms of happiness is instant gratification, and it's external happiness that we find outside of ourselves. Unfortunately, it can also distract you from making the necessary changes to get the result you deserve. One of the easiest ways to do this is to purchase a new handbag, buy a new aftershave, or buy things you don't need.

It can act as a distraction and that instant feeling of happiness and satisfaction doesn't last as long as finding a deeper source of joy. You purchase something, feel good, become tired of that item, and need something else to buy. You need to stick something else on the credit card and potentially get into more debt.

The best form of happiness is happiness that comes from within. It's internal happiness and you've heard it before, but are you tapping into it? Going within and finding happiness from the inside out rather than the outside? Being happy with who you are as a person, your good and bad traits, and making peace with yourself? Change becomes easier to manage when you have a deep well of happiness emanating from inside you. I know that we're spiritual beings having a human experience and have all that we need within ourselves. We don't need external factors to make us happy. Everything we need is within us.

We can tap into our source of happiness, richness, goodness, and abundance. It's just like breathing; you don't have to think about it, and you have a right to feel happy. A deep sense of happiness comes from having a purpose, having a mission greater than oneself, and feeling alive and ready to take on any challenge.

Principle 9: Be Grateful for Your Current Situation

It doesn't matter where we find ourselves in life. We can find something to improve on. Life is forever expanding, changing, dying, and birthing. Every living organism is doing the same. The single most important state of mind that you can practice is love and gratitude for everything in your life, starting from when you wake up.

The very situation that we deem challenging now, later in time, will turn out to be a blessing. Being in a state of gratitude is like being in heaven and it fosters peace, harmony, and big-picture thinking. It allows us to see all perspectives and truths regarding our circumstances and brings us into the present moment of the here and the now. Right now, how many challenges, issues, or changes do you have to make? Not many, right? You're reading this book, so occasionally, your mind might drift away from the task, but you bring yourself back to the here and now. That's an essential gift of gratitude, a feeling of presence, aliveness, connection, and peace.

If you haven't heard of Dr. John Demartini, his teachings are deep, meaningful, and practical. One of his rituals every morning, before he gets out of bed, is to recite all the things he is grateful for in his life. He doesn't get out of bed until a tear of gratitude appears for all he has in his life. Can you imagine doing that every morning? This is one of the reasons he is an amazing man and positively impacts so many people. I like to take short moments throughout the day to acknowledge how amazing life is and breathe deeply

113

into my lungs and give thanks. Even 30 seconds of doing this can bring us into gratitude.

Perhaps your chosen path involves maintaining a gratitude journal, a nightly ritual where you reflect upon life's blessings before sleep. By integrating this practice into your daily routine, the seeds of gratitude bloom into a harvest of increased happiness, enhanced well-being, and profound serenity. I encourage you to persist in your journey of self-expansion, approaching challenges with an optimistic outlook, and faithfully applying the principles we've discussed. With these actions as your compass, anticipate the emergence of miracles on this remarkable voyage of self-discovery—an embodiment of the miraculous power within, waiting to transform your life.

"Your life is your own miracle in the making. Embrace it, nurture it, and let it unfold in magnificent ways."

~ Unknown

CHAPTER NINE

Gratitude vs. Fear

By Annette Forsythe

Have you ever experienced the fear of the unknown or felt threatened by some unusual circumstance you couldn't identify? Fear is that ugly emotion that lets us know there is a physical, emotional, or psychological threat nearby. It could be real or imagined, but it always feels real regardless.

As children, many of us experienced the fear of monsters under the bed or in the closet. We would be frightened by unknown experiences or trying new things. Anything that made us feel like we were in danger was off limits.

As we grow older, that sense of alarm tends to follow us. It might not be the monsters under our bed, but we do have our own demons that follow us. Behold our patterns, the ones that hold us back from moving forward. Some of our fears could be considered silly or irrational. For example, I am terrified of spiders. Logically, I am 1,000 times larger than one, so what exactly is there to be so afraid of? But those legs! And you know, sometimes they are large and strong enough to move furniture! Just saying!

If you think about it, how have your fears held you back and kept you from being everything you are meant to be?

Fear can show itself in so many ways. Physical reactions can make you numb or paralyze you. When I was a young mom, I fractured my ankle. I required surgery and was hospitalized for a week. Before I could be discharged, I had to be able to walk up and down the stairs on crutches. I had never used crutches before, and I had absolutely no idea what to expect. So here I am, in a giant boot in the hospital with crutches in hand, and the physical therapist says, "Okay, go up the stairs . . ." Are you kidding me! Tears were running down my face, but I reached down deep and did it, one step at a time. When she said to come down, I froze! I just stood there. I tried to move. Believe me. It just wasn't going to happen. Long story short, I failed the stairs and had to stay another night. The next day was still awful, and I did it with a lot of determination: determination and the need to get back home. I have never experienced a paralyzing fear like that since. Once I faced the fear, I was so grateful that I had a home I would be able to navigate around in, my two little girls who would love me for me, and my father and husband who would care for me and keep me safe.

Emotional fear comes from being vulnerable or leading with your heart. We expose ourselves when our heart is involved. We have to trust that we will be safe and not hurt. That requires courage. When relationships are new, there is a fear of the newness until we know more about the relationship, be it personal or professional. Uncertainty equates to fear or insecurity. When you are already feeling unworthy, it is hard to leave space for a relationship to be what you hope for. You are forgoing any predisposed notions of what could be and doing yourself a huge disservice.

I believe that insecurity adds fear to our lives. Some ridiculous things go through my head. I am afraid that no one will show up at my funeral and that my daughters won't know how to find where I have been laid to rest. Or that they will live so far away that I will be forgotten. I fear that I won't leave a legacy or an impact on my world. I fear I am not important to my family, that they care more about other relatives or family friends than me. I fear that I am not enough to keep my husband from returning to his old ways and drinking again. I always worry that I am not worthy, that I will never lose weight and that I won't fit in a casket. These are only the tip of the iceberg. I fell in my office last week. The entire staff came over to help me. I stopped them all because of that fear they would feel I was heavy.

When I become vulnerable to the fear of my insecurities, I reach a whole new level of crazy. Who thinks like this?! It would be my guess there is more at work here than just me. When we are in the midst of these vulnerable moments, we forget that we have the choice to put them to rest. When we give our insecurities our emotions, we make them real. If we strengthen our belief in ourselves, we can put them to sleep. We all have the power to avoid being a victim to our thoughts. Unsurprisingly, gratitude, confidence, and belief play significant roles here.

Uncertainty can undoubtedly add to psychological fear. Thinking small and a lack of faith in oneself is a terrible combination.

Since moving to the new office, my business partner and I have caught ourselves in moments of reacting in fear and thinking small. Admittedly, moving a business is a big deal and presents much to be fearful of. Moving a business amid a global pandemic is absolute lunacy because the restrictions in New Jersey were intense compared to other states in America. We planted the seeds for growth and now we need to remember to be patient as we wait for them to grow. It takes time. We have done the work. Now we have to wait for the results to come. This is where our gratitude comes in to remind us how blessed we are to be here doing what we love and adding value to the world.

When you take enormous risks, there can be overwhelming fear. It would help if you carried a solid belief to survive. But even with strong faith, fear can rear its head. It is all a roller coaster of emotions and if you choose to be grateful and have confidence, you will succeed. What you focus on, you find, and fear can skew that focus. That puts the power in what you fear and not what you want.

There are multiple levels of fear that show up every day in my physical therapy office. The fear of pain can hold our patients back and slow their recovery. There is also the fear of being broken and the fear of rehabilitation (the unknown). We see these fears in people of all ages. It's just perfectly human behavior. Our job is to build rapport; let them know they are safe, help them realize that there might be some pain, but they will be able to work through it and get to the other side, toward their desired outcomes. They are not broken, just temporarily indisposed. Their success is the result of the choice they make to recover. We stand beside them and encourage them to want the most out of their therapy.

No one wants to feel broken, including me. As I learn to navigate my diagnosis of rheumatoid arthritis, I have battled fear. My point of reference for people who had this diagnosis was found in wheelchairs and their limbs were gnarled. I know times have changed, as well as all the available treatments. Movement is very important, yet movement is what causes me pain. Sometimes, you have to call on your determination to get to the courage and strength that comes from perseverance. I am so grateful to be around a group of professionals who are there to encourage and challenge me every step of the way. If I gave into that fear of pain, I would have a very debilitated future in front of me.

One thing is for sure these days. We have all shared the chronic trauma of the COVID virus. The past two years have found many of us isolated and completely changed our life approaches. There has never been a pandemic in our lifetime before. Therefore, there are no past experiences with which to reference. We haven't had answers to many of our questions because most solutions are unknown. I can't imagine the extent of the anxiety for those of us who are more certainty driven.

As we navigate getting back to our old lives, there is still a fear of being around people. Mask, no mask? Inside, outside? How many people? Who's vaccinated, who's not? So many questions before we even take the first step out. How do we move forward with so much uncertainty? As someone who is high risk and still extremely cautious, this is a big problem for me.

I trust myself but find it difficult to trust anyone else. If you are not wearing a mask, are you vaccinated? Or do you not believe in the virus? My husband and I were recently invited to a communion party. Was it safe to be in a church? How crowded would it be? I was full of trepidation, but I knew it would be okay. We were going to be with family. I believe we are all carrying more scars than any of us realize. For now, I am genuinely grateful that my immediate family has managed to stay COVID-free for the past two years.

You have probably noticed that I have thrown measures of gratitude in from time to time. What do fear and gratitude have to do with each other? The answer is simple. When you are grateful, you have confidence that everything is a gift, even pain. There is an appreciation and a greater commitment to relationships or tasks. Gratitude gives you a sense of confidence that everything will be alright. The knowledge that you have enough, that you are enough, and that there is nothing to fear but fear itself.

When you are thankful, it is easier to recognize that things happen for you, not to you. Instead of being fearful, you see the value of every experience in your life.

When you are alone with your thoughts, does fear feed your patterns? It can be challenging to stand up to our patterns, and anxiety can establish a stronghold when we are afraid of what we might find. Heck, we may even find that we are lovable and are good enough if we do that. Unfortunately, all the positive affirmations in the world aren't strong enough to make those feelings less awkward and difficult to believe. So, what are we afraid of? If we take away the fear, patterns, and excuses, we might have to accept our worth. Just imagine!

So, is it fear that holds us back from our greatness? Let's be clear. Fear is a natural emotion. It's just that when you're grateful, you can assure yourself that the fear is only a temporary detail.

If my business partner and I had given in to our fear, where would we be? Would Netcong PT even still exist anymore? This is where we go back to courage. Gratitude can feed our ability to face things we are afraid of. Think about where history has led us. Imagine what life would look like if our ancestors didn't take chances. If you don't believe and take chances on any relationship, whether personal or otherwise, what sort of stagnation would you find? I think life would feel robotic.

The fear of failure is human. Being aware of our reactions and responses to any situation is the first step in addressing the patterns that make us less than great. When we can recognize and stop the habit and go inside ourselves, we find our greatness.

Living in a state of gratitude places your focus on everything good, on all the blessings and gifts in your life, lives filled with abundance and understanding. It is difficult to be fearful if your heart is peaceful and full of love. I believe that I have learned to live in a state of gratitude. My family and friends' blessings in my life, what I have, and the beauty around me never go unnoticed. My gratitude and my beliefs give me a greater appreciation for every day, allowing me to bring my best self to everything I do, even when I step out of my comfort and take risks. Look for opportunities to challenge yourself. It is truly liberating.

"The greatest miracle is not in achieving the extraordinary, but in recognizing the miraculous within the ordinary."

~ Unknown

CHAPTER TEN

Create Connection
By John Spender

The Universe, Spirit, God, or whatever you want to call it, sends us signs to let us know whether we are on the right path toward creating miracles. If you are aware, you'll see the signs in your environment. We are, after all, very much one with our surroundings and we can connect with the energy in our environment.

One afternoon, I had driven to Canggu from Sanur, Bali, where I lived, to help organize a Toastmasters meeting. I opened the seat to my scooter to grab the prizes when I turned around to see something fall out of the sky. It plummeted on the ground inches from my feet. I looked down and saw a dead finch. It had dropped dead, barely missing me as it fell to the earth. I instantly thought that was a little creepy, hardly a sign that I could pretend had never happened. A few dogs came over, wagging their tails with happy demeanors. Perhaps this wasn't a bad omen.

The next day, I did a little research online. I discovered that a dead bird symbolizes the end of a relationship or the new beginning of a paradigm of new relationships, not just intimate ones. It was nice to get affirmation that I'm heading along the right path after ending a five-month relationship that was quite draining.

No more than a week later, I was sitting in an Italian ice cream parlor in Sanur, chatting with a friend, when suddenly I felt a splat on my head. Sure enough, a bird had shat in my hair! My friend burst into laughter. It must have been a big bird because there was a fair amount of poop to wash out of my hair. Everyone knows that if a bird craps on you, you can expect good luck to come your way. We left the parlor still laughing when I saw yet another dead bird, a large white dove. After a little more research, my findings confirmed that a series of dead birds is a common indication that new relationships are forming, and how you show up is also changing. After doing a lot of volunteer community work, the strange thing was that my past patterns of having anxiety attacks when in new social environments began to fade away.

An old saying states that if an unusual incident happens once, it's bound to happen a second time, and if it occurs twice, it's highly likely to happen a third time. Sure enough, a few days after seeing the second dead bird, I again randomly spotted a third dead bird. I was in northern Bali, close to the old capital Singaraja, showing my friend Carat Waterfall. We were walking down this steep path when I saw a small flying lizard gliding through the air. When it landed, I pounced on it and took a photo of this amazing reptile. A small dead bird was lying there on the ground, and I knew right away that this was a significant moment and that my life was, indeed, moving in a positive direction. You know you are your own miracle when you are doing things that you love and are feeling good doing it. Every event in our life is a potential miracle. Life becomes less about "Is this the right or wrong choice?" and more about "Does this make my spirit soar?" If you can answer the latter question with a yes, then keep doing it. If not, you can make a simple adjustment. At the same time, you are allowing your environment to guide you. Signs don't always come from nature. Other times it could be from a conversation you are having. It helps to set clear intentions about what you seek confirmation on.

While working on my first documentary about the gift of adversity, I was experiencing a significant moment of self-doubt about what to do next. I asked God, "If I'm meant to make this film, show me a sign." I instantly felt better, took a shower, and played indoor cricket in Dalung, about 40 minutes from where I lived in Bali.

One of the boys had brought his American friend along, who had never watched a cricket game before. I was briefly introduced to Adam before focusing on the match. We won the game convincingly and afterward, the team returned to the local pub for a few beers. I don't usually go as I prefer not to drink alcohol, but feeling good after the win, I decided to celebrate with my teammates. At the pub I noticed that Adam wasn't drinking alcohol either. We started chatting and it turned out that he was house-sitting and looking after a friend's dog. Naturally, I asked him what he does. "I'm a film producer," he replied. Talk about divine timing. Adam became my advisor on what action steps I needed to take next! Those that know, know that we are connected to infinite intelligence. All we need to do is connect with it.

In the 1950s, Carl Jung, a Swiss psychologist, was formally recognized as coining the term synchronicity, which means a series of meaningful coincidences that occur randomly yet seem to be meaningfully related. For example, you start thinking about a friend that you haven't seen in a while and, sure enough, you bump into them. That's synchronicity. After talking to your friend, you might discuss that you are looking for more work, and they know someone looking for exactly the type of service you provide. If you look deeply enough, you'll see that random events are synchronistic to you or the other person in some way, that we are all part of a collective consciousness, and when in harmony with our existence, life happens for us in the most empowering way.

Jung worked with many patients over his career, and one of his most famous stories was of working with an intelligent woman hiding behind her intellectual abilities without having an emotional connection with what she was talking about. Yet, she always had an answer for everything. Jung was listening to her express a vivid dream from the night before; she was gifted a piece of jewelry in the form of a golden scarab. At the same time, Jung heard a tapping at the window behind him. As he turned around, he saw that it was a reasonably large insect that wanted to enter the room.

"How strange," he thought. Jung opened the window immediately and caught the bug as it flew inside. It was a scarabaeid beetle and its gold-green color looked almost identical to the golden scarab beetle in his client's dream. He handed the beetle to his client and said, "'Here is your scarab." Jung is quoted as saying that this synchronicity burst her bubble of intellectual protection and she began to open up and experience a deeper connection with life. That's a perfect example of a seemingly random event that, upon reflection, had a deeper synchronistic meaning.

Recently, I traveled with two friends from Sedona, Arizona, to St. George, Utah. Adam was driving, Casey was in the passenger seat, and I was in the back seat. We were all doing Dr. Wayne Dyer's Ah Meditation, the sound of creation. It was during this 20-minute session that I heard Adam yell out and Casey say, "Wow, you just missed a deer!" I looked through the side window and, sure enough, saw a deer bolting into the bush with a terrified look. Casey, having a grounded connection to synchronicity, instantly looked up the symbolic meaning of almost hitting a deer. She read the definition to Adam, as he was the one who had nearly hit the thing. I remember the explanation she read and feeling like it was also relevant to my life.

The spiritual meaning outlined that this was indeed a favorable omen and not a negative one, as one might think. It was a sign of abundance—an abundance through working with a group of people rather than doing things the hard way or by yourself. There was an emphasis on joining a team or working as a group to reach your fullest potential. Since I was in a meditative state, I asked my higher self if this was also a message for me and to show me a clear sign. About 45 minutes passed, and the deer incident was in the back of my mind. We stopped at a gas station and I went to the bathroom. As I was at the urinal, I saw the day and month of my birth—the 22/09/—clearly etched into the metal water pipe above the urinal. That's when you know you are in the flow of life where synchronicities are an almost everyday occurrence if we are open to connecting with them. ·

When we arrived in St. George for Lenny Evans's Bliss Retreat, I was excited as I had heard so much about this retreat that Lenny had been running for several years. Casey had organized me to lead an 11-minute breathing session for all the trainers speaking at the retreat. It was such an emotional, moving experience of connection as Lenny facilitated a gratitude circle for all the speakers, with many of the shares being deep and personal. Most of the people in the group had known each other for a few years. The level of connection, empathy, and vulnerability was powerful, and it was the perfect segue to my breathing session. The session went well. Everyone loved it, and there were hugs before we left to prepare for the opening day. Casey also asked if I would like to speak about my vision-creation process, which was an awesome surprise. There were 50-odd people in attendance, and I was excited to share the stage with my good friend. The energy in the room was heartfelt and grounded, creating ease with which to share and connect with a receptive group.

Once my share concluded, I had people coming up to connect or ask to sign a copy of the last book I had collated. It was fun and surreal all at once. One of these new connections is a fantastic woman with a professional background in scriptwriting, and she offered to help me with the movie documentary I'm making. This experience highlighted even more than synchronicities are miracles in action. The ancient Chinese text of the Dow De Ching states, "Do nothing and leave nothing undone." That is a great verse to meditate and reflect on. The only questions you need to focus on are, does it feel good? And will others benefit from this decision? Then, as the old saying goes, follow your bliss.

The challenges we face include maintaining the mental state of bliss where life flows effortlessly. The funky stuff only really appears when we are feeling disempowered. One of the ways to create this state is to live in the present moment, and the best way is through your breath. By focusing on your breathing, you are experiencing the present moment now, the living essence of life. If you think about it, we can last weeks without food, maybe months. We can survive without water for days, maybe weeks. But try holding your breath for a minute; it can feel like an eternity. Without breath, we are nothing. The air we breathe is a miracle, but how many people treat it that way? Breathing is our birthright, and it happens automatically. When you take this miracle and breathe consciously, your connection with your body, mind, nature, and creation becomes seamless. The body begins to heal itself. Your mind becomes clear and focused. Nature communicates with you; you exist in harmony and can manifest your desires at lightning speed. In short, you become a sourcer, connected to the Source of creation.

I first began to understand the power of breathing when I read Sonia Choquette's book, Traveling at the Speed of Love. One of the breathing techniques she shared to help develop the sixth sense was box breathing, where you breathe in through your nose for four seconds, hold, breath out gently through your nose for four seconds, and hold for four seconds, repeating this over again for four minutes. This simple yet powerful process will have you centered in the present moment in four minutes or less. There is also something magical and grounded about the number four. Think about it for a moment. Four is the number and symbol for many things in western culture. For example, there are four cardinal points: North, South, East, and West. There are four phases of the moon. There are four seasons: Autumn, Winter, Spring, and Summer. There are four elements: earth, air, fire, and water. The four states of matter: solid, liquid, gaseous, and igneous. The four known physical forces: nuclear force, radiate force, electromagnetic force, and the force of gravitation—the four blood groups: O, A, B, and AB. The four-leaf clover is a lucky symbol and represents Hope, Faith, Love, and Luck. One of the most valuable symbols of four is the four conditions that make life on Earth possible. It's the right distance from the Sun, it's protected from harmful solar radiation by its magnetic field, it's kept warm by an insulating atmosphere, and it has the right chemical ingredients for life, including water and carbon. The number four also symbolizes building a solid foundation to create and manifest one's life.

My first practical use of this breathing technique was to overcome fear, particularly concerning public speaking. When I first started public speaking, I was terrified, and it felt like I would have a heart attack each time I spoke before an audience. I remember my first public speaking opportunity was at Mission Australia in Sydney, teaching the homeless and disadvantaged personal development skills in a two-hour class. My preparation was solid. I had never done anything like that before, as my background was in landscaping. This was in 2010, and I clearly remember driving into the city and being unable to breathe or focus. However, once I did the box breathing, I could concentrate, drive to the venue, and connect with people in real need. Teaching those classes was something I did for over three months, and it was a great way to build my confidence and develop my love for supporting people that wanted to change.

Of course, you don't have to wait for an emotionally significant event to start practicing box breathing. This breathing routine also includes circular breathing, which is fantastic for healing. I recently discovered circular breathing through a friend, Samantha Hoogenboom, who teaches breathing classes in Ubud. Her sessions go for an hour, and although it can be hard work, the healing and balancing of the body and its organs feel fantastic. It's an easy process done through the mouth. You breathe in through the mouth and imagine your breath traveling down the front of your body, and you instantly exhale through your mouth, imagining the breath traveling up your spine. I remember feeling pains in my lower intestine for a few weeks and by the end of the session, the pain had disappeared completely.

As beneficial as circular breathing is, finding an hour each day for this method can be challenging, and it requires more discipline if you are going to be consistent. Therefore, I have combined these breathing techniques to create an eleven-minute breathing session that will have you in your natural state of peace, ease, and grace, and connected to Source. In addition, I do breathing exercises every day to maintain a peaceful state of mind.

Step 1: Begin with four minutes of circular breathing. Remember to breathe through your mouth and imagine the breath traveling down the front of your body. And then you instantly exhale through your mouth, imagining the breath traveling up your spine and straight back to inhaling your breath down the front of your body. The idea is to oxygenate your body and exhale all the toxins you breathe in. Deep inhales and exhales are best, breathing in from your stomach and exhaling out and straight back to a deep inhale, repeating for four minutes. This will also warm up your body if you are in a cold climate.

Step 2: Without skipping a beat, it's straight into box breathing next. As I mentioned, breathe in through your nose for four seconds, hold for four seconds, breath out gently through your nose for four seconds, and hold for four seconds, repeating this for four minutes. The inhales through your nose are done gently and deeply, and the exhales through the nose are subtle, barely feeling your breath on the top lip.

Step 3: Finally, there is extended box breathing. Breathe in through your nose for four seconds, hold for eight seconds, and then breathe out gently through your nose for eight seconds, and hold for four seconds. Repeat this for three minutes. In the end, you may want to repeat some affirmations in your new empowered state of peace, connection, and abundance. The three I like to use are:

1. I am the universe and the universe is me.
2. I send love to my fears; my fears are places within me that await my love.

3. I always attract the highest and best in all people.
4. I'm always in the right place at the right time to have magical experiences.

A timing app on your phone is handy, and you can set bells or chimes to ring at the end of each interval. For example, I use insighttimer.com, a meditation app that allows you to use a timer with cool bells/gongs that sound after each interval of the three breathing sets.

Do this breathing exercise every day for 21 days and watch your connection with the world change. If you want to deepen your practice, do this exercise twice a day - once in the morning and once in the evening - and journal the subtle differences you notice. For example, was it challenging to hold your breath in the beginning? Did you have a lot of mind chatter? How peaceful did you feel afterward?

Reflection is a powerful difference we have from every other living creature. Use it and watch yourself gain more clarity, focus, and a deeper understanding of who you are.

Making empowering choices from a big-picture perspective is about connecting to the flow of who you are, what you desire, and how it feels. Monitoring your feelings enables you to practice the art of discernment, and it helps to understand the law of focus, which has four parts:

1. What you focus on, you find.
2. What you focus on seems real.
3. What you focus on grows.
4. What you focus on, you become.

I discovered this way of thinking from the teachings of Rod Hairston, featured in the documentary I'm producing. Knowing the law of focus drives home the points of knowing what you want and visualizing how you want it. Now you have a vision, and your choices and decisions must align with that vision through your actions. That will give you purpose. It can be as easy as that to start living a life of miracles.

Bear in mind, a single moment of clarity can serve as the catalyst for an entirely new existence. Embrace the notion of exploring your envisioned reality, searching within for the desires that resonate. As your self-awareness deepens, your rapport with the world around you flourishes. Within the realm of seemingly commonplace occurrences lie hidden signs waiting to be deciphered—a process that sets the stage for synchronicities, the threads that weave the fabric of miracles. Remember, we are intertwined, intrinsic elements of the expansive universe—both presently existing and forever entwined within the tapestry of all that has been and will be.

"**Miracles happen when you believe in the power of your dreams and take inspired action towards their manifestation.**"

~ Unknown

CHAPTER ELEVEN

---∘◦C∕◦∘---

Challenge Is a Gift

By Annette Forsythe

I can't tell you how many countless times I have heard the saying, "Anything worth having is worth working hard for."

It's such a broad statement, yet it carries so much meaning. It doesn't refer to just physical activity but to every part of your life—the way you take care of yourself, the goals you make, your relationships, your beliefs, the list goes on. It's natural to want to follow the path of least resistance. After all, it's easy and doesn't take much thought. Just follow the yellow brick road. But "the yellow brick road" isn't real. It's not that simple.

In reality, everyday life is challenging. We have 86,400 seconds in a day to make the day count. Every one of them is filled with decisions that get you through the day. It's so automatic we don't even think about it. We keep moving through, not even realizing what we are accomplishing—decision-making in the broadest sense.

Then, there's the good stuff. The choices and challenges that require some effort. The ones that give you goals to achieve and make you uncomfortable. The ones that come from having a vision. We have goals for our fitness, health, jobs, and finances, testing the limits of our physical strength and mental ability. Visions set the ultimate goals and challenges in front of us. They give our brains something to focus on and set us up for success.

We're not meant to roll through the days, although sometimes that seems like a good idea. We are all programmed for greatness;

motivation and determination are what get us there. But let's not also forget about vision. It's like using your imagination with great intentions. Because our potential is limitless. How big are your dreams?

When you're young, your beliefs are laid out for you. Next, our parents determine our paths. But as we get older, we take the reins and start making our way.

Our challenges become our choices. We get to decide how big or how little, how hard or how easy. Do you want to go for the brass ring or take the easy path? Our visions are the driving force behind these decisions.

For me, I have written down a vision for every part of my life. I read them regularly and keep them close to my heart, protected like a child. They are mine and do not need to be judged by anyone. These visions give me focus, and what you focus on, you find.

Visions offer a guidance system, a path for your brain to follow and direct your focus. They should make you feel uncomfortable and that's where growth happens. When you write down a vision, you should picture it as already done. It should be written in the present tense and focus on your desired outcomes.

My vision to help others manifested when I got a job working for a physician. Then it expanded to be part of an office where patients came first instead of the bottom line. I didn't have any details. I just knew it would happen. Soon after, a conversation started with one of my coworkers. She was a physical therapist. Originally, she proposed a job opportunity. She would stay with the physician and I would do all the groundwork for her new office as her employee. I turned down that proposal and countered with my own. I told her I would gladly take on the risk of a new business as her partner. And so, the vision was about to come alive. We were open for patients within three months. The bonus of this story is that I also found a way to earn the income that could support my girls and I if we ever needed it.

In all honesty, though, I never once felt that we would fail. Even when times have been dark, my faith knew we would never fail. After all, how could we when we did things with honest intentions and for the right reasons? That was 22 years ago and we are still alive and well.

My gift from that experience was twofold. Not only did I find a way to support my family, but I also discovered my strength and ability to build a career. Our potential in life is only as strong as our beliefs. We all have gifts to offer this world, and we can't let fear hold us back, making it challenging. It's a gift to be able to push our limits.

We must be ready to face the challenges in every aspect of our lives. People with chronic health issues are challenged every day, always striving for the perfect balance between being broken and learning to live a productive, happy life. It's a battle not to let the negativity of a diagnosis hold you back from living life. Do the work, empower yourself with knowledge, find the way to overcome the apparent symptoms, and make the necessary changes to your lifestyle. Move through your pain, get stronger, and create your quality of life. A better quality of life is a precious gift to give yourself.

Someone fighting cancer faces the challenge of literally fighting for their life. Probably the greatest challenge they will ever meet. I have always found that my greatest tests have brought me the greatest gifts. We get to fight. We get to look inside ourselves and be grateful for the experience. We get to find our courage and show our strength. We get to make choices.

Our challenges, the ones we create and the ones life hands us, bring opportunities. We get to experience them, and we get to make choices about what outcome we are seeking. When we pay attention, we will not only see the "silver lining" in each. We will find unexpected opportunities for greatness.

I believe that with every challenge placed in front of us, there is a lesson to be learned. Each of these lessons is a gift. These are not the kinds of gifts that come wrapped with a bow. They are much more exquisite. They are life gifts. The advantages of patience and understanding, the skills of experience and learning, and the gifts of integrity and choice are just a few, yet each of these gifts is what makes us who we are.

Every challenge is an opportunity to grow and be our best selves. Our responses to these moments are a test of our emotions. When faced with a difficult situation, how do you respond? Do you make it all about you, or do you stop and think about what the other side needs? There are lessons to be learned from everything we do and how we react.

My father became disabled when I was 13. He was managing my uncle's rock quarry when the bucket of a crane fell on him and almost decapitated him. It crushed his legs, injuring the veins and causing deep vein thrombosis. That led to the first of many pulmonary embolisms over the next several years. Dad was quite fragile after that accident. A few more accidents happened until Dad was forced into "retirement," when he was only in his early fifties.

Our lives took a drastic turn when this happened. It would be almost three years later that he finally received his disability. My dad exhausted every source of income they had in that period, cashing in insurance policies and all their savings. My mother could stretch a dollar further than anyone I have ever known. There was always a hot meal on the table and food in the refrigerator. We did have extra and love was abundant. They did everything they could to make my life as normal as possible. Although my sister was already away at college at this point, it was hard for her not to be home and see everything going on for herself.

When I turned 14 and became eligible to work, I got a job at the local supermarket. I handed my paycheck over to Dad for the household every week. He would give me money for gas and a little for spending. It was a family effort. We all did our part. That was just the way it was.

The first time I drove a car was to rush my dad to the hospital. He had collapsed while throwing another blood clot. After that, his hospitalizations were regular, and I spent many hours by the bedside with my mom as a teenager. She had her license and was terrified to drive. So, we had to depend on the kindness of neighbors until I got my license and could take over . . .

Since time stands still for no one, things still had to get done around the house. Dad's activities were very restricted. So I learned to do many things like rotate tires and lay sod. There were a few occasions when Dad wished he had a son, and I proved to him I was the next best thing, and so was my sister when she was home. I'd be lying if I said it was easy. Tears were shed. It was a scary time. But as they say, where there's a will, there's a way, and we all did our best to find the way. Don't forget, we learned our strength from some incredible women.

This was a challenging time for all of us. I didn't realize this at the time; we all had to dig deep. As I look back, I can see how blessed we were to live through this. We appreciated that we were a tight-knit family who would stick together. There was strength in our numbers, learning to work together at things beyond our skill level and to cherish each day as if it might be Dad's last.

Dad had to accept the changes in his life and we had to challenge ourselves past our emotional and physical limits. And we did, bless him. For someone who was given only a few years to live, Dad saw 93 years and got to hold all his great-grandchildren. By the way, all those "manly job" skills I learned have been tools in my toolbox ever since. I learned to be strong and self-sufficient during those years. I learned how to tighten my belt when finances get tight. I learned never to fear trying new things. All skills that certainly helped me through the challenges awaiting me in my adult life.

Mom was the glue that held us together. She took such good care of my father. She was the one who made sure he made all his doctor appointments and had all the medical equipment he needed. She sat for endless hours by his bedside so he wouldn't be alone in the hospital. She was there to advocate for him every day. Nothing was too much. I am confident that witnessing my mom taking care of my dad gave me the courage to understand that my husband's alcoholism was an illness and that I needed to stand by his side and let him borrow my power.

My life's journey has certainly had its share of challenges. Some of little consequence and others that have been life altering. My mom always said, "You can knock on any door . . ." With that thought in mind, my responses to these moments have shown me how courageous I can be. Life experiences have taught me that I have everything I need within me. I can do anything I need or want when I set my mind to it as long as I believe. Just keep the emotional responses out of the way and stand behind what you know to be true.

Maybe belief in oneself is the most consequential challenge anyone can face. It's a tall order and very easy to discount. Here's the thing, though—if we don't have belief in ourselves, how can we manifest our visions or make anything happen? We have it all in us! I am capable and you are capable of anything we want. So, find your courage, take a deep breath, and take the first step. It really gets easier after that, once we get past the anticipation and fear. Then we can realize there is nothing to fear but the fear itself.

The gifts we get are twofold with every obstacle that comes before us. First, we get to take on life and everything it offers, allowing us to test our courage and strength. Second, we get to make our desired outcomes become a reality. We can't fail when we believe. These lessons move us forward to the challenges yet to come.

We haven't talked about the challenges we face against ourselves when we face our inner demons, our limiting beliefs. The things we tell ourselves can be rather brutal. Significant emotional events and patterns we inherit usually hold responsibility here. When I heard all the weight comments made toward me as a young teen, their impact lived right under the surface. When anything came up, those were the first words I heard in my head. I couldn't possibly be worthy of any success. So, I walked around full of self-doubt. I shake my head now when I look back because I have had many successes. I must remember to graciously accept the acknowledgment and praise, no matter how awkward it makes me feel. I smile and nod, yet in my head, I have a completely different conversation. How can someone who has done all the things I do be worthless?

Even after all the work and changes I have made in the past several years, this one is still a problem. There have been so many lightbulb moments as I have been peeling away layers of the negative talk. I say positive affirmations every day, but I still have an issue accepting that I deserve good things. That I am worthwhile. I will tell you. I will not give up the fight to stand confident in my skin. That is my gift from self-doubt. I continue to choose to be healthy. My QTR, quality time remaining is going to rock!

Looking back, everything I have faced to this point has brought me to where I am today. Digging deep to fight for my marriage and learning to accept my husband's illness. Giving him the belief that, as a recovering alcoholic, he can be the man I know he is. Forgiving him for the heartache he caused, yet loving him deeper than ever after 41 years. And looking forward to all the adventures ahead as we approach retirement.

Together, we have raised four daughters (with only one bathroom, I might add). We gave everything and did our best; however, their childhoods were riddled with addiction and unemployment. Nevertheless, they have grown to be incredible women I respect and admire. Plus, they have made us proud grandparents.

I decided to take our financial welfare to the next level, and made several decisions that would never allow others to pull the rug out from under us again. I started a business that has kept a roof over our heads and paid the bills. I was able to build my confidence in knowing I could take care of myself and my family, a much-needed boost to my morale. It's the ace I could keep in my back pocket for if and when I needed it.

Keeping this business going for 22 years has been a blessing. Ownership lawsuits, blizzards, hurricanes, fires, and pandemics have done their best to shut us down. But we persevered and found ways to keep us going. We believed in the services we provided and had the confidence to make it happen.

In an earlier chapter, I wrote about the importance of health, especially as we make our way through our daily obligations. It's hard to do when your body isn't at 100% and doesn't cooperate. Since 2019, I have broken an ankle and a rib; I have had pneumonia five times; and I have been diagnosed with rheumatoid arthritis and other chronic autoimmune issues. In my perfectly unprofessional opinion, this has all resulted from extreme stress, thanks to living through a pandemic, being in isolation and quarantine, losing a beloved brother, functioning in a state of self-despair, and keeping a business afloat while moving the company to stand a chance at survival. My point for sharing this is to remind everyone that as we face life's challenging moments, we must pay attention and take care of our health, or there is a solid chance we might lose it. There are gifts in this as well because we get to tap into our strength for courage and survival.

I have shared some raw personal stories throughout these chapters—many based on the challenges I have faced and overcome. I won't pretend there haven't been moments of self-doubt. But once I got past my initial emotional breakdown and self-imposed limitations, I was able to own them and do what needed to be done. I am grateful for the lessons I have learned from every one of these hardships, these experiences. I am who I am because of them.

So, say thank you and be grateful. Appreciate the fact that every day is a gift. Every one of those 86,400 seconds is an opportunity to be awesome. Every experience lived and those yet to come should be treasured. They are what has gotten us to this point—accepting the fact that we are all human, that none of us are perfect. We are imperfect beings and deserve a little grace for any less-than-stellar moments as long as we learn from our experiences. So put those limiting beliefs aside and embrace the fact that you have everything you need within you right now. You can accomplish anything you want with belief, focus, and vision.

"You are capable of creating miracles in your life by embracing your inner strength, resilience, and unwavering determination."

~ Unknown

CHAPTER TWELVE

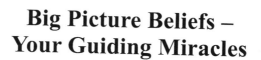

Big Picture Beliefs –
Your Guiding Miracles

By John Spender

O ur beliefs create our reality, which is simple in concept. The only problem, though, is that most people don't know their beliefs and where they come from. This is why people can feel like victims of their circumstances, often surprised by their current reality. Our lives are a collection of past actions driven by our unconscious beliefs held over a prolonged period. Most of our beliefs come from our parents and the people we spend the most time with. It's not until we begin to question the thoughts and beliefs we are living that our life can change for the better.

Certain beliefs in life are empowering and can be the guiding light for your life. Being your own miracle requires a high level of personal responsibility for understanding yourself and why you do what you do. It doesn't matter how far you have gone down the wrong road. It's never too late to choose a different route and start fresh. Adopting "big-picture beliefs" is equivalent to casting a grand vision for your life. It begins with believing that anything is possible and that you deserve to live the life you want. Moving toward big-picture beliefs is to walk the path of miracles, the path where, step by step, anything is possible.

Big-picture beliefs are essentially overarching, fundamental beliefs and values that shape a person's perspective and guide their actions in life. These beliefs are often related to a person's sense of purpose and core values. Big-picture beliefs can vary from person to person, but they tend to be deeply held convictions that shape a person's worldview and guide their choices. When people live in alignment with their big-picture beliefs, they tend to feel a sense of purpose, fulfillment, and direction in life. When I was in my twenties, I used to believe that you needed to work hard to generate a lot of money or even a sustainable income. This is what I saw my parents do. I often heard, "Look how well so-and-so is doing. He works so hard!" If you listen to Gary Vaynerchuk, he often talks about the grind and out-hustling your competition.

Well, I worked hard in my landscaping business for many years and experienced success at a high level, winning many large council contracts over the years. I also experienced burnout, having a nervous breakdown at just 24. Fast forward to today and I have a team of people working for me. I mostly work four hours a day with the remainder of my day focusing on my passion of reading and writing. Today, I believe you don't have to work hard for money and I also have many friends that live this way as well. I live a balanced life that is aligned with my purpose and passion. Following my big-picture beliefs has helped me live a more fulfilling life, and I believe that it can do the same for you.

The first big-picture belief I invite you to explore is that you are not just your body, thoughts, and feelings. You are a spiritual being having a human experience. Your meat suit is temporary, but your spirit is eternal. It's the thinker of your thoughts and the feeler of your emotions.

An excellent way to test this is to simply observe your thoughts, listen to the voice in your mind, and notice how it slows down as soon as you become the silent witness. For example, you may hear a voice saying you're hungry or thirsty. That's the mind. The mind often lives in absolutes; either this or nothing at all. You have probably heard the saying "My way or the highway." Well, the mind is almost like a two-year-old child and will run wild if you let it. To live a peaceful and productive life, we must learn to control the mind or it will control us.

Our emotions often derive from our thoughts, beliefs, and judgments. Even though it can be difficult to control what we feel consciously, we can bring our consciousness, awareness, and point of focus to our emotions. If, for example, you are feeling stressed, overwhelmed, or anxious, you can stop, sit, take a few deep breaths, and bring your attention to the feeling without judgment and the sensation will soon dissipate.

Once you practice this and develop a deeper connection with your soul, it becomes easier to make decisions that are in harmony with your greater good, and you can become more aligned with your sense of purpose. Your life will start to have a greater depth of meaning and direction, breeding contentment and a longer-lasting level of happiness. The more you do this, the more you will naturally trust your feelings and what you should do with your life. When you are on purpose and aligned with the direction you need to take next, it'll feel like a knowing, like you know what it is; there can also be signs. Oftentimes, though, it can bring up fear of the unknown as well. For example, you'll meet people doing what you are passionate about, or you may get the opportunity to try something new. You can be confident that it will take you out of your comfort zone, but you'll be rewarded with a bigger version of yourself.

When I sold my landscaping business, I just knew it was the right thing to do. My friends and family at the time didn't think it was a good idea, trying to dissuade me from making that decision. My mum was almost begging me to reconsider and she has been right about many things in my life, but in this case, I knew that I needed to trust my intuition. That's the richness of life, dying to the old and embracing the new. Living from your soul is to be your own miracle.

Big picture belief number two is that you choose your parents before birth. This was a big one for me as I went through several significant emotional events as a child. Adopting this belief helped me see the divine nature and order in things, that miracles can hide in bad things, and that there is a gift in everything if we can open our hearts to see them. For example, I used to hold onto resentments toward my parents for different things that happened in my life. Thinking if I hadn't experienced these events, my life would be better off. After working on myself I discovered that I was viewing the situation from an unequal perspective. I initially only recognized the pain and suffering caused and not the positives that came from the experience. We live in a world of duality; good - bad, hot - cold, day - night, sad - happy, the list goes on and on. After calibrating my emotional events I was able to uncover the gifts that those moments gave me. I can see how those moments build strength, resilience, and compassion into my character allowing me to empathize with others that have been through similar challenges. It certainly prepared me for my career as a coach a decade later.

Believing that, on some level, you choose your parents is incredibly empowering. It takes you from victimhood and powerlessness to one's circumstances to a situation of choice to serve a higher purpose and deeper meaning for your life. It removes the disempowering belief that I would be okay if my parents were different. This belief lets us accept that everything happens for a reason and for the greater good. Every time we point a finger at someone, three fingers point right back at us. I like to ask, "What is the gift in this situation?" or "What good can come from this that I'm not seeing now?"

A man who I had the honor of hearing speak on many occasions, Dr. Wayne Dyer, is known as the "Father of motivation" and is the author of some thirty books many of which were New York Times Best sellers in the Self-Help genre. One of the many phrases of his that has stuck with me is "When you change the way you look at things, the things you look at change." When I changed the way I viewed the relationship with my parents, the relationship deepened and I was curious about what things happened to them as children. As a result, my perspective expanded and I had a better understanding of who they are as people doing the best they could with what they knew at the time. Miracles are possible when we see events from several perspectives, not just our own.

The third big-picture belief is that you create your reality. You are the ship's captain, the master of your destiny, and the director of your movie. Ultimately you get to choose the direction of your life, which is very empowering. This means you can change your current circumstances and create a new reality. Naturally, it won't happen overnight, but the belief enables you to take control of your life. You are ultimately responsible for your life and no one else's. Getting caught in the blame game is a real trap that will prevent you from reaching your highest potential. Owning your life can be a little scary, and it's almost like dying to the little version of ourselves and allowing our greatness to shine throughout with the old and in with the new. However, taking ownership and responsibility for our actions is the answer and is a massive step forward in developing trust in oneself. This starts with what we habitually do every day.

If there is an area of your life you aren't happy with, the power is in your hands to change it. For example, if you are struggling with your finances and in debt, or maybe you have had a few bad months in your business. Either way, one of the fastest ways to turn anything around is to be grateful for what you already have. See the abundance on the supermarket shelves, the abundance of beautiful homes, or new cars in the streets. A favorite of mine is to walk into a furniture store or electronics store and imagine all the things I would buy, as if I already had the money, and then give thanks. As a minimalist, I'll probably never buy those things, but it will get me into the prosperity mindset. Feeling worthy of more brings it to you when you are of service to others and consistently seek to add value to your clients or workplace. Be a giver. Look for ways to be kind to your fellow humans and you'll find it easier to summon the courage to create your desired life.

Often, it's a matter of self-reflection and examining how we show up every day. How are you choosing to get out of bed every morning? I encourage you to begin the day with gratitude as you open your eyes. Creating a morning routine was a game-changer for me. Getting out of bed with a clear intention of doing yoga, reading, self-reiki, affirmations, walking, meditation, box breathing, or a chakra meditation has grounded me with clarity on how I want to start the day. I haven't missed a day in over 1,000 days when I haven't done at least five of the above exercises, and on average, I do at least seven of them over a day. I use Insighttimer to track and measure what I do daily. Most successful business owners track and measure their finances, so why not do the same with your well-being? We lose everything if we lose our health, so it's necessary to look after our body, our temple. Taking responsibility for my health and wealth were two of the biggest game changes for me to live a life of my choosing. Naturally, I'm course-correcting as I go, and having a morning routine has created a solid foundation for my own areas of my life that I would like to improve.

Big picture belief number four is that every situation has a benefit, no matter how bad, painful, and unfair it may seem at the time. The gift will be revealed if you open your heart long enough to accept the situation. I know it can seem counterintuitive, and the question pops up, "What is the benefit of having cancer?" My friend's client was a 15-year-old girl with cancer, and when he asked her about the benefit of having the disease, she was taken aback by the question. After some time, she said that she was drifting away from her family before the diagnosis, becoming very self-centered and mixing with the wrong crowd at school. The benefit of cancer for her was that the illness had brought her closer to her family again. She also mentioned having a new appreciation for life and clarity on what matters for her moving forward. Last I heard, her cancer was in remission, and she was getting involved in a humanitarian project. If this young girl wasn't open to seeing the benefit of her situation, she might have never healed and missed the opportunity to make a difference in other people's lives.

When we see the benefit, we receive the gift of any scenario life throws at us. It's empowering to believe that no matter where life's journey takes you or your situation, there is a benefit just below the surface waiting to shine its light on you. The question is, are you ready and open to receiving it?

Big-picture belief number five is you don't need fixing. That's right. You don't need fixing, because you are not broken, and whatever you're going through now won't last forever. We all need a reminder of our magnificence. The news tells us how terrible the world is and creates negative conditioning and programming. Doing what you enjoy daily is one of the easiest ways to remind yourself of perfection. Unfortunately, watching the news and keeping yourself updated creates a paradigm of fear programmed deep into your subconscious mind. Most of the time, we don't get the complete story anyway. The stories are told from a limited perspective and don't give the viewer both sides of the drama.

By reducing the hours you watch TV and instead focusing on activities you can do with friends, you will bring absolute joy, happiness, and laughter to your life. There is a time in everyone's life to heal wounded aspects of ourselves, but that does not mean you are broken. What we focus on expands, meaning that if you focus on limited parts of yourself and the world, you will get more of the same in your life. In addition, what we resist persists, especially with emotions and anxieties. For example, imagine swimming in a pool and trying to push down a beach ball underwater. The harder you try to submerge the ball, the more it wants to pop back up, almost like a jack in the box.

The same is true with emotions that we don't want to feel, let alone express. I had a client who would avoid feeling sad like the plague. After doing many processes with her, she could release the emotion's power. In essence, feelings are neither good nor bad, it is the meaning we place on them that makes them so. Sure, a certain set of emotions feels light and brings happiness to our lives. Equally, some feelings feel heavy and unpleasant, bringing gloom to our lives. The idea is to feel them, express them, and move on. Focus on activities that give you a sense of timelessness and create movement through exercise. The idea is not to get stuck on either side of the polarities of emotions.

It takes awareness to be centered and constantly remind ourselves of our magnificence. Then we can begin to trust the universe and tap into our connection with everything, including our decision-making process on what we want with our life. It can be hard to trust our inner calling when the news tells us there is so much to fear. It can be challenging to know who to trust when things aren't going our way.

Even salt looks like sugar, right? We need to trust ourselves to get back into the flow of life, back into the flow that synchronizes and synergizes with our needs and desires, where manifestations happen almost instantly and making the right decision is easy. Trust is a key factor in choosing the right career, partner, and anything we want in this life. Faith over fear is needed. If life gives you salt, put it on your chips! If life gives you sugar, put it in your tea!

There is good and bad in all things; the secret is to utilize them and have them work in our favor. Everything is here to serve us if we open our hearts to see the gift. No matter what other well-meaning people say, trust that the universe will conspire to help you once you know what you want to do. The right people and opportunities will be open to your will, desire, and drive. When we know what we want, what we wish for will seek us.

Making Big-Picture Beliefs Work for You

When you adopt big-picture beliefs, you can expand your awareness of what is possible for your life and what is most important rather than wondering, "Is this career right for me?" With big-picture beliefs, the question changes to, "How is this career serving me?" You can bring passion and love to anything you do, and in many cases, it all comes down to the questions we ask ourselves.

Big-picture beliefs empower you to seek challenges that test you to become a bigger and better version of yourself, to learn, develop, and create opportunities that inspire others to do the same. We will always have some form of challenge on this journey we call life, and that's a good scenario to have as that can motivate us to become more expanded in our reality. When you move toward a vision that inspires you, the challenges can become fulfilling to overcome. The obstacles become something to experience on the way to your goal rather than being in the way. There is a natural richness in this type of living where you become more in the process.

Here are some tips on how to make big-picture beliefs work for you:

- Be clear about your big-picture beliefs: Start by identifying your core values, beliefs, and vision for your life. Then write them down and revisit them often to stay aligned with your goals.

- Use visualization techniques: Imagine living your desired life and achieving your goals. Visualization can help you stay focused, motivated, and positive.

- Take consistent action: Break down your big-picture beliefs into small, achievable goals and take action consistently. Celebrate your wins and learn from your failures.

- Surround yourself with like-minded individuals: Connect with people who share your vision and support your goals. Surrounding yourself with a supportive community can help you stay motivated and accountable.

- Stay positive and resilient: Maintain a positive outlook and develop resilience when facing challenges and setbacks. Use challenges as opportunities for growth and learning.

- Continuously learn and grow: Invest in your personal and professional development by learning new skills and knowledge that align with your big-picture beliefs.

- Practice self-care: Take care of yourself physically, mentally, and emotionally to maintain energy and motivation. Prioritize rest, exercise, healthy eating, and activities that bring you joy and fulfillment.

By applying these strategies consistently, you can make big-picture beliefs work for you and create a fulfilling and meaningful life.

Adopting big-picture beliefs can be a powerful tool for creating your desired life and becoming your own miracle. It starts with identifying your core values, beliefs, and vision for your life and then taking consistent, inspired action toward achieving that goal.

As your journey of becoming your own miracle unfolds, remain receptive to the unfolding of growth and transformation. Embrace the prospect of acquiring fresh knowledge, stretching the boundaries of your understanding, and greeting challenges as gateways to progress. Devote resources to both your personal and professional advancement, while prioritizing self-nurturing to sustain your vigor and enthusiasm.

The voyage toward embracing overarching beliefs demands patience, continuous exertion, and unwavering dedication. Yet, armed with resilience and a steadfast resolve, you possess the capacity to construct a life harmonious with your core principles and loftiest ambitions—thus embodying the miracle that stems from your own efforts and unwavering commitment.

You really can do anything that your heart calls you to do!

"The true miracle is not in changing external circumstances, but in transforming your own perception and response to them."

~ Unknown

CHAPTER THIRTEEN

Forgiveness

By Annette Forsythe

From the pages of our favorite novels to our own tense holiday dinners, family feuds are all around us. We have all likely experienced discord in our own relationships. But how often do you ask to be forgiven or tell someone you forgive them? Are they simply words, or do you have any thoughts or reasoning behind them? The dictionary defines forgiveness as a conscious decision to release anger or hurt, let go, or pardon an offender. I prefer to see forgiveness as giving up hope for a better past. It's a great way to remember you can't go back, that you must keep moving forward.

The past six years have taught me about forgiveness at a whole new level. It's a word often used too lightly. True forgiveness takes work and thoughtfulness. I came to appreciate taking responsibility for my actions, even when I thought I didn't have any. "What? I am the one who's been wronged. How is any of that my fault?" Just think about it. When you point a finger at someone, there are three more pointing right back at you.

I have already mentioned my mentor and friend, Rod Hairston. My connection to him comes through Growth-U. Rod challenges our team with so many models for growth. One of them turned out to be one of the greatest gifts I have received from the community. It's called the A-U-A model, and I use it all the time. Accept, understand, and appreciate: three simple words that showed me the path to the kind of forgiveness that gives your heart true peace.

The first step is acceptance. You must learn to accept the reality of the situation or action you want to forgive. No embellishments, just the facts. The truth of the problem comes with answering all the questions: who, what, when, where, why, and how. When you paint the whole picture and see the circumstances which led there, you get better insight into the infraction.

Then comes understanding, and I don't mean just understanding what may have happened. I mean understanding the other side. Put yourself in their shoes. What was their driving force? This requires you to think outside of yourself. Only after you have made yourself aware can you accept and understand. It's not making excuses for someone's behavior; it's understanding where the behavior is coming from and why.

Once that work is done, you can begin to appreciate how or why something happened. You are ready for forgiveness only when you have gone through this process. Be clear; this work is not for the other party but for you. This extra effort allows you to move on with your life without the burden of pain and resentment. I believe we have all had moments of forgiving and being forgiven. I know I certainly have.

When I met my husband, my foolish heart believed we would live a fairy tale. It would be so simple: boy meets girl, they date, they fall in love and marry, they have a family, and everyone lives happily ever after!

Well, when I took my rose-colored glasses off, maybe we had half a fairy tale. We were very much in love in the beginning, and we live happily now—but the middle part was pretty gritty.

We met when I was in college. He had already graduated and he was a working professional. I worked part time at a pub where he was one of the regulars. The truth is, it was anything but love at first sight. Our love story began when the sarcastic banter turned to flirting and we became best friends. We were definitely products of the '70s, living large and playing hard. We were kids and we were fearless about pushing the limits. Doesn't everyone do that in college?

My husband was transferred to Maryland right before our wedding. So, he went north to Maryland and I went south to Fort Lauderdale with my parents until the big day. We spent our honeymoon moving and getting our first taste of married life. My husband would come home from work and we would have drinks before dinner as we talked about our days.

It wasn't long before I realized he was drinking three beers for every one I had. This would be a problem, and as it continued, it became our dirty little secret.

A few months later, we were transferred again to New Jersey. I was pregnant with our first child. My husband continued to drink enough for both of us. That's how the story went on for many years. Somehow, he never got the memo: it was time to stop being an outlaw and grow up.

When my two older daughters were little, it was easy to hide our reality. But as they grew older and the younger girls were born, it wasn't so simple. Their level of awareness was much greater than I ever gave them credit for. My husband wasn't always a fun drunk. You never knew what side of him was going to show up. And no matter what we did as a family, he made sure he did his share of pregaming.

Suffice it to say that I spent the first 20 years of my marriage walking on eggshells. There were so many arguments, so many tears, and so many excuses. As hard as it was to admit, I was married to a fully functioning alcoholic. We were well known in our community. I had to protect my family. No one could know what was happening behind closed doors. I thought I was protecting my daughters; I was very naïve. They knew everything. It took years for me to realize his drinking had its effect on all of us.

You're probably wondering why I didn't leave. I couldn't. I didn't know how I would take care of my daughters; I was a stay-at-home mom and a super volunteer in our town. I didn't have my own income, and I was completely dependent on him. Before, I had never considered that I had given up my independence by living my dream of being home to raise my family.

The truth is, I really didn't want to leave. I knew the man I'd fallen in love with was still there somewhere. A bottle of vodka wouldn't take away my dreams or our happy memories. This was also about the time when my sister kicked my ass and told me to stop being a victim. This was the part where I had to put on my big girl pants, and soon a business was born. My success would allow me to care for my daughters and myself. This was my choice.

Then my husband had a severe health crisis. I prayed this could be the answer. He had a choice: stop drinking or die. His treatment plan included medication that could kill him if he consumed alcohol. But let's be real, that did not go smoothly. He continued to drink and eventually became so toxic he had to be hospitalized.

What the hell! What more was in store for us? God answered my prayers, finally, and put His fear into my husband. That was the beginning of 12 years of sobriety, 12 of the most glorious years my family ever had. The man I married was back. We celebrated births, graduations, weddings, and everything else in between. I was living my best life with the man I loved by my side.

Have you ever heard of Murphy's Law? Now that things were going so smoothly, my friend Murphy managed to show up and do us all in. We got the news, a lot of news, all at one time. First, my husband's youngest brother suddenly passed away the same day we found out our youngest daughter had thyroid cancer. Not long after those shocks, we lost our first grandchild to a stillbirth.

Those days were some of the most gut-wrenching I have ever experienced. I was filled with fear and heartache I didn't even know could exist. Imagine the impact it had on someone inclined toward self-medicating.

I thought I saw signs, but how could that be? Twelve years of hard work to stay sober was worth too much. I would mention my suspicions to my daughters, and then we would all agree that it would be impossible!

Impossible until I started finding the empty pints around the house. The evidence that proved my worst nightmare had come true. And just like that, we were headed right back to the life I swore I would never live again. By ignoring the signs, I was slipping back into my enabling behavior without realizing it.

My dad came to visit us that summer. He was not in good health and spent his entire visit in and out of the hospital. My husband would see him at lunch and I would leave work early, get there by 2:00, and stay until 10:00 or 11:00 p.m. It presented the best scenario for someone who had relapsed. He did not have to hide because I was never home. When I did get home, he was sound asleep.

When I started finding the bottles, I was so angry, but still so protective that I couldn't tell anyone. When my dad was finally healthy enough to return to his home, my sister came to get him. It had been a stressful day, and thanks to my husband, it became an ugly evening too. After a drunken outburst in front of my family, I was horrified with him. I finally asked the one question that had haunted me for over 30 years: what would he choose, me and our marriage or the booze? There is a reason they tell you never to ask questions you don't want the answer to.

I moved out of our marriage the same day my family returned home to Florida. We lived separate lives under the same roof for almost two years. I drove around with half of my belongings in my car. I made purchases for a "new home," having everything delivered to my office. I meant what I said, and I never lived that other life again.

This is when I found the community that has become my chosen family. When I met my friend and mentor, Rod Hairston, I learned the A-U-A model and put it to use. I was invited to a retreat in Austin for Growth-U. Our entire group was there equipped with our growth mindset. a growth mindset. I wanted this new experience and needed a chance to work on myself and clear my head. When I left home, I didn't know if I'd be returning. I had a cashier's check for $12,000 in my purse and was ready to start over if needed.

Do I stay? Do I go? Can I forgive? I had decisions to make. I was pointing fingers and placing blame. Then I realized I had a shared responsibility in this nightmare. That concept was a shocker, but I had to own my part. I was the one who had enabled this behavior all these years; I had to admit I was codependent.

I knew this trip would be life-changing the moment I walked in the door. I found the independent girl I used to be. I was no longer a victim. I was strong and capable. Here is where my greatest journey and learning experience began. I began concentrating on healing my heart. If we had any chance at reconciliation, I needed to find a way to forgive him. I needed to believe in him and be prepared for the rocky journey ahead.

If I was going to find forgiveness, I had to find a way to accept what was happening. My husband is an alcoholic, and he has an illness. When those bad moments happen or the hurtful words fly, it's the addiction, not his heart. Could I accept this, or was it just a convenient excuse to be mean? My rational mind knows that we are not our patterns, but our routines and habits are hard to break. I know that firsthand. If bad habits were easy to overcome, I would be a size two.

Once I got through the process of accepting his illness, I had to understand it. I had to truly understand that his alcoholism was an illness and that neither of us had power over it. I had to realize that his behaviors were the result of his addiction. With understanding,

I could appreciate what he was up against. That the effort it would take for him to become sober was not a straight path. That all he could promise was one day at a time. Only then could I find a way toward forgiveness like I have.

This story has several layers. The first was my husband's ordeal and learning to forgive him. But while this was happening, as I hid our reality from our young daughters, something else happened. In my efforts to protect them, I was causing them pain. I never saw the domino effect my behavior had on them. Whenever there was a fallout between my husband and me, I turned around and found reasons to be angry with my girls. It wasn't really anger. It was because I was hurt. This was a pattern I identified years later, and I am not proud of it. In the big picture, the daughters I cherish became collateral damage from my dependency on their father. Don't get me wrong; it wasn't all sadness. There were many joyful times in our life and a lot of love and laughter. But like everything else, the ugly stands out the most.

As hard as this might be to believe, this realization of my part in our dysfunction never occurred to me until recently. I know I was far from perfect, but I also did the best I could, given our circumstances. Making amends with my girls is a work in progress. I own my responsibility here. As their mom, I should have protected them better. God willing, they will forgive me in their own time and way. I can accept, understand, and appreciate why they are angry with me. In the meantime, I just keep pouring out my love to them.

Now for the third layer of this story. Between my husband and my daughters, I carry a lot of guilt. I feel that I should have done more and been more, that I should have been able to fix all of our problems. I'm a mom. That's what we do. In my eyes, I came up short, and so I blamed myself for most of my family's issues. There were moments I wished I could give back and do over. Instead, I needed to find a way to A-U-A myself.

The challenging part was finding a way to forgive myself for all my perceived shortcomings. This is a large order of business and still a work in progress. It's hard to step away from Italian guilt. But, I'll repeat it, I did the best I could to give my kids a good life despite my husband's addiction.

We all carry scars, guilt, and shame. I am blessed that my husband is aware of his responsibility. He owns that he is the reason for my fear and that he has broken my trust. There were so many lies! The fear of a relapse is ever present and so human. However, when you truly forgive, you also have to be willing to allow the space for people to be who you expect them to be.

If you say the do, you have to do the do, and that's easier said than done. I forgive my husband, yet every day, fear plays games with my head. When it gets too much to handle, I blurt out accusing thoughts without thinking. The hurt on his face kills me. He may be understanding, but I am not. I apologize when this happens. The whole scenario leaves me with a lot of guilt for doubting him, but my heart knows he is doing his best and I am only human.

The good news is that now my husband and I have a relationship where we talk about everything with understanding and grace. I am genuinely proud of his efforts to live a sober life led by a higher power. He realizes that he doesn't want to be that other person anymore. He has embraced a new lifestyle that makes him happy enough not to want to go back to drinking.

The man remains the love of my life. I accept his illness and I understand it takes work. I appreciate every day God gives us that is free from alcohol. I have forgiven the past and look forward to everything that lies ahead for us. I am blessed he is comfortable enough to allow me to share our story in the hope that someone may need to hear it. Recovery is not a straight path. There have been slips along the way. These are the moments that have fueled his determination to stay sober. And in turn, I have to tame my response to those slips because he is also human.

My daughters are still working out all their feelings, but we love them like crazy and will be there when they are ready to talk it out.

As for me, learning to forgive myself has been some of the hardest work I have done. Guilt is heavy baggage. It has taken years and more tears than I care to count to get to a healthy place. We all have our moments, both good and bad. I had to allow myself the vulnerability to admit I was flawed, I was fallible. I had to separate from the emotions and not let those actions define me. I had to forgive myself, accept my humanness, and be confident that I had done my best.

Even though I am responsible for my own actions, I also acknowledge that everything that went wrong in our life was a shared responsibility and not just my fault. My growth journey has led me to a place where I can accept myself for who I am. I refuse to spend one more minute of my QTR (quality time remaining) feeling bad that I have come up short. I am enough as I am. That is a lesson I wish I could share with everyone who has ever felt they are not good enough.

"You hold the power to turn impossibilities into possibilities. Believe in yourself, trust the journey, and let miracles unfold."

~ Unknown

CHAPTER FOURTEEN

Transformation Is a Journey
By Annette Forsythe

In any journey, there are many roads to take and obstacles to overcome. However, what gets us to our final destination is the freedom to choose our way . . .

When I began my journey, I was broken. My self-esteem was at its lowest and my home life was a disaster. I felt like the only reason I deserved to be involved with the Growth-U community was simply because I was alive, not because I was worthy.

Transformation and growth do not happen overnight, and to call it a journey is almost an understatement. This journey is all-encompassing, and the destination is always in front of us. But there is no "there," and we keep moving towards new goals. It's the cycle of growth.

My journey has been incredible. It all started with a Facebook post. I had no idea what I was getting myself into. "Find your inner badass." That simple statement changed my whole world. I happened to see it when my marriage was falling apart. I was at a crossroads and not sure what to do next. Then I saw it—find your inner badass. My first reaction was, "I am a badass! Well, I used to be a badass. Maybe I could be a badass?" So, I made a phone call. That was when I found Growth-U and my transformation began.

Was I meant to remain a victim of a sorrowful life, or could I be the hero of my own happy life and thrive? So far, it felt like life was happening to me, not for me. If I wanted a change, I had to be the change. It was time to take charge and write the rest of my story, no matter what played out at home. I was my story's future, and how that future played out was up to my own courage and self-belief.

I needed to begin an education in personal growth. It has been the hardest yet most satisfying challenge I have ever experienced. It has involved candidly analyzing every aspect of my being: thinking, changing, parting with the comfort of my old habits, and stepping into the unknown. I had to stop pointing fingers and blaming my circumstances on others. Instead, I had to own it all.

I put my full trust in the process and started giving from my heart and soul, knowing it would all come back to me tenfold. I am living by the laws of the universe and training my brain to focus on my desired outcomes. I possess the power to be my own success story. Just remember, things don't just happen. There are old patterns to break and new beliefs to be found. Being kind to yourself and changing your self-talk is imperative. You have to dig deep and find the courage that lives within you and take a leap of faith. You are the key to your success and fairy-tale ending. I have taken my newfound tools and enriched my being, allowing me to live my best life, one filled with love and gratitude.

I enrolled in program after program to better myself. I began finding my inner strength. I cheered through the excitement of change and danced through the realization that this would be hard work. That hard work led me to my transformation and a new identity. In the blink of an eye, the whole process began again because growth is a continuous cycle. I have been on this journey for the last six years, and I am grateful to say I am still a work in progress. I have conquered so many aspects of my world—for example, my career, finances, communication, and energy have all been fine-tuned with my visions—and there is still so much work to do.

With faith and belief, I have grown a thriving business that continuously reinvents itself to keep giving the best care to our patients. There is so much comfort in redefining my wealth. The daily practice of gratitude, taking inventory, and recognizing all the ways in which my life is blessed reminds me how wealthy I really am. I have learned not only to listen but to really hear when I am spoken to. I have also found the courage to speak what's in my heart, and not just what I think people want to hear. My energy levels are no longer weighed down with all the negative self-talk and old patterns that left me feeling worthless. I recite positive affirmations every day. I am always fine-tuning my visions so my brain has a target, and my mind will take me there. I take total responsibility for my actions, knowing my actions and words are the only things I have control over. Most importantly I have learned to forgive myself and others and move on, appreciating that we are all human. The intentions were good. Hanging on to old hurt is just unproductive. I deserve to be free from those burdens.

I tease that my husband came with a small wooden ironing board. It is actually perfectly sized for someone short like me. I guess I came with my baggage too. I talked about growing up as an Italian earlier in the book. Food was the answer to everything. My weight issues began at a very early age and have been the bane of my existence.

I have realized that I have used my excess weight as protection. A safe comfort layer that took the blows every time. You see, food never hurt me. The people I loved did. The irony of the whole mess is that this "protection" has really caused my deepest pain. It's exhausting living a life anticipating when the next round of humiliation will hit.

Here I am, 65 years old and still dodging bullets. When I look in the mirror, I cringe at the reflection looking back. I don't see the badass woman who gets things done; I see a little girl who doesn't believe she's worth anything because she has spent a lifetime disappointing her family and, most importantly, herself.

There were so many patterns and so much fear. Fear of being hurt, fear of failing, and the fear of letting myself down again. Imagine who I could be if I were to rid myself of the fear and conditioning that has been so deeply embedded into me. What is the identity I want? Am I the fat girl? Or am I the woman who leads with her heart to improve the world?

I have never been afraid of hard work and sincerely want these answers. But unfortunately, I am the one who has to find them. There is a journey of introspection here. I have acted on the words of noted writers Brene Brown, Michael Singer, and my friend, psychotherapist Catherine Duca. I have been encouraged by my respected friend Rod Hairston. I have even surveyed esteemed colleagues and friends for their insight.

There is one truth I am sure of: I can no longer accept a life filled with regret, shame, and disappointment. Life is too precious to waste on unwanted patterns and self-destruction. I have come to recognize that my focus has been directed toward what I don't want: everything I fear.

Who would I be? There would be confidence, peace, and joy. I would be comfortable in my whole skin for the first time. I would even fit in. When I put the patterns to rest, my story will inspire as it plays out organically.

I have never really bought into the "inner child" concept. Instead, I have compartmentalized my life—many of the boxes hold successes, but there's one secret box that's buried and tries to control my state. She is the child who just wanted to be loved, accepted, nurtured, and encouraged to do great things. She is the one who has been the voice in my head. You know, the one who's there to put you down. So, I have acknowledged the patterns and now understand the depth of this inner conflict.

When I presented a survey asking for accounts of people's first impressions of me, I was shocked. I expected to read comments that noted some of my assets and expected a lot of "isn't it a shame about her appearance?" Just like I'd heard when I was younger. But that's not what happened. They saw me! (I even checked to see if they were talking about someone else in the room.) They saw love and kindness, and they saw nurturing and loyalty. I asked for brutal honesty and I received beauty and no judgment.

It's up to me to nurture this little girl inside my head. I am the one who needs to cherish her and approve. She is the foundation for the person I am. A friend asked me, "Would you talk to your children the way you talk to yourself?"

My answer came quickly—"NEVER!" I found that question so powerful, and it stunned me into opening my eyes. Yes, there were some sad stories in my past, but it has been me who has kept them alive. It seems I have left the grown-up me in need of love and nurturing.

It is now time to remember those three fingers that point back at me every time I try to pass the buck. I have blamed circumstances and past hurt for my patterns all these years. It is time to own up to my responsibility and make the most of my time on this Earth.

The value I add and the love I give are overshadowed by my own doing. It is my choice how I want things to play out. I have everything I need within me to change this, and I'll borrow the courage to do so from the people who see me.

There are times when I feel like the many faces of Eve. I learned at a young age that I could adapt the way I needed to present myself and hide behind a mask. "Put a smile on that face!" "Do not let them see you were crying!" I swallowed so many emotions and those masks could cover up a lot of pain.

It's hard to admit that my pain has been self-inflicted. Emotional responses can lead you down a slippery path. Put on the face, show up how you're supposed to be, and hide your reality—lessons not to be soon forgotten. Never let them see you sweat. It doesn't matter how you feel. Hide it at all costs. Do what's expected of you.

After a while, it just becomes natural, and at 65 years old, you could even call me a professional. I have controlled the part of me the world knows, and I am very selective of who I let in. The world knows her as real, confident, and successful, a real badass, and I have safely hidden the part of her that holds pain and longs to be recognized as worthwhile.

I have forever been a people pleaser. If I make everyone happy, I've done my job and I don't get hurt. It is a lot of pressure. When I fail, it's a downward spiral into the depths of self-loathing. From the beginning, food was my source of comfort, so I blindly self-soothe. Then when it all sinks in, disappointment follows. I cause my most destructive pain while trying to avoid pain. It's pretty messed up.

In all these years, I have been able to forgive those who have hurt me. All except for one, the ringleader: me. I have understood the words and actions of others came from a place of love. It was what they knew, and what they thought would encourage me to be my ideal self. But unfortunately, it has taken a pandemic to make me take the time for reflection, introspection, and the vulnerability to be brutally honest with myself, just as I asked for from my friends and colleagues.

I began my growth journey almost six years ago, before my sixtieth birthday. The first lessons learned involved a vision, the cycle of growth, and a quote. "There is no there." Our work to improve ourselves and our service is never done.

My marriage was about to end, and I was lost. Years of his alcoholism and my self-worth issues did not make a good combination. I had to figure out where I was going because I learned I had a choice. Who knew?

All the compartmentalized boxes in my life were being exposed and opened. Patterns were fought and put to rest. Every trip through the growth cycle was like peeling another layer off an onion; with each layer came more belief, courage, and peace. "There is no 'there'" became one of the greatest gifts I have ever received, along with the freedom to choose. The old patterns are still dormant and looking for every opportunity to rear their heads. But I am more harmonious with it and always on the lookout.

This journey has been a process. I've been ticking the "easy" stuff off the list. And now, these trips through the cycle are more internal. We are getting to the real nitty gritty: honesty, vulnerability, and courage.

As the core of my layers was finally being exposed, my desire to understand became stronger than my desire to hide. I had the work, tools, and the courage to eventually figure out who I was from the inside out. I had to face my fears of what I might find along the way.

Discoveries have unfolded that I didn't expect. I have acknowledged weaknesses and uncovered patterns that have done more harm than good. I have woken up and am seeing details I was blind to. I have learned to respect those three fingers that point back at you when you point a finger elsewhere. I understand that taking responsibility is up to me and that forgiveness is more for me than for my offenders. So that I may let it go, I must be the one to let go.

Let's be real; the easiest person to lie to is yourself. Maybe that's why I hate lies—because I can lie to myself. It hasn't served me well at all. I have forgiven all the hurt and the pain. I know the actions were out of love. As odd as it sounds, guilt is a powerful tool in my family. As for my marriage to an on-again, off-again alcoholic, well, maybe I am just a slow learner, and it's taken almost 40 years to realize that as much as he talked about my weight gain, he did his share of sabotaging me. I believe it was subconscious; he just wanted me to feel as bad about myself as he did about himself. Yes, he's human too.

It worked because I gave in to it. Patterns repeat themselves, and I realize my daughters were caught in our patterns, as much as it hurts to admit it. I never realized this until I began shedding my masks. Apparently, I made the girls wear them too. As misery loves company, let's all feel awful.

That Italian upbringing is still predominant: hide your feelings, swallow the hurt, put on the face. Everyone must see the perfect picture, and we must keep up the act at all costs. I have spent a good bit of these growth years beating myself up for my less-than-stellar days. And I believe, from the bottom of my heart, that I did some things right, because they have all grown up to become incredible women. Some of that was me, as well as many great memories and experiences. Despite multiple layoffs, financial hardships, and the dirty-little-secret addiction, we gave everything we could.

My sincerest efforts have gone into accepting this part of our family history and behavior. I take full responsibility for all my actions and any shame or humiliation I have caused my loved ones. I did the best I could, as did my family before me. But unfortunately, we hurt the ones we love, and we are all perfectly imperfect humans. It wasn't easy, and there were four of them and only one of me.

My growth journey has brought out discoveries every day. I started out looking for one answer and uncovered a lifetime of patterns. But unfortunately, there is no "there," and as I unfold this new courageous identity, the next cycle is just around the corner.

As my husband continues his recovery, I accept and forgive his actions. He has an illness. No matter where we end up when this chapter is complete, I know I will be alright. I have everything I need within me, and I have a lot of fight left in me. I have plenty to be proud of. I am enough just as I am.

That little girl, she grew up to be a badass lady that makes shit happen. Unfortunately, she was so busy taking care of everything else, she forgot to take care of herself. Just a few more shifts and she'll have it all under control. For now, I will walk tall and hold my head up high, facing those truths that are too hard to admit.

The more I showed up, the stronger I got. And my belief in myself begins to look different. I have visions to guide me and an underlying belief that I am already there. I am manifesting happiness and a new sense of confidence. The more my confidence grows, the more I change. I am rediscovering the girl I used to be all over again, the girl who took any challenge head on with no fear—you know, a real badass.

I wear my heart on my sleeve. I have extremely high expectations of myself and find it difficult to let go of any of my mistakes. Sounds crazy, doesn't it? Yet I am willing to overlook and forgive everyone else around me. I am living a double standard.

Who knew you went through different phases when you wanted to make lasting changes in your life? In the beginning, it was all exhilarating. It seems so easy. "I got this! What's so hard about this?" In reality, you have no idea of what you don't know. You're ready to celebrate because this effort feels like a piece of cake. Just wait; the best is yet to come.

Then about a week or so in, you start to struggle. You are not as enthusiastic as you were. This changing business is harder than you thought. Here is where you realize this whole endeavor will take some work. You have a battle going on in your mind. Things can go back to how they were, which is the easy way with the comfort of old patterns, or you can keep working at creating new habits, uncomfortable and pressing ahead.

Believe it or not, this realization is actually the happy part. It's time to celebrate because a change is coming. When the shift starts, this is when you begin to transform and make these new behaviors yours. Your actions become so natural that you don't even realize it. You have created a new you! In the blink of an eye, before you even notice, you've taken the next step toward a new identity and start the whole process all over again. You have to go through the entire cycle for lasting change. If you don't have the identity to support your changes, the transformation won't last. There is no "there!" We just keep growing.

Every virtue discussed in this book is part of the process. Every aspect of the journey requires digging deep and remembering. First, you need courage and gratitude. Next, you must remember to add value to the world because you get back what you give. You just have to pay attention. Finally, you need to have belief and a willingness to grow and do the work. Take on those old patterns and stop the comfort they bring you. Push yourself to step out of your comfort zone and stop doing things the way you always have. Create new behaviors and be productive. Write down those visions, use your imagination to see the life you want to live, and go for it. You really can do this; it's all inside of you.

I have been asked if sharing these stories has left me feeling exposed. Well, they certainly are vulnerable, and the exposure is welcomed if my experiences help even one person. When we go through life, we can feel very alone when facing some of our challenges. Maybe someone won't feel so lonely if they read my experiences. Perhaps these stories can give someone hope that they, too, can find their inner badass!

We get but one life. We all deserve for it to be sensational, and it's up to us to make it that way. The best part is that we already have everything we need inside of us. We get to make the choices that move us forward. I have shared my most vulnerable moments. Well, all but one—I still find it too embarrassing. Let's just say it involved throwing and actually hitting a target (a first); small, heavy objects were kept out of my reach for a while. What can I say? I'm human. I will tell you, though, that it has taken every experience I have lived through to get exactly where I am now. I know I am exactly where I should be and am filled with gratitude for every one of those 86,400 seconds each day.

"Believe you can and you're halfway there."

~ Theodore Roosevelt

CHAPTER FIFTEEN

The Power of a Mindset Open to Miracles

By John Spender

Throughout the book we have shared our insights and stories and there is no way either us would be where we are today without a mindset open to miracles. It's an attitude that an incredible force can bring about transformative and positive changes in one's life. Let's reflect on the basis that a mindset refers to the collection of thoughts, and beliefs, that shape an individual's perception of the world and themselves.

When someone possesses a mindset open to miracles, they approach life with a sense of wonder, hope, and receptiveness to the extraordinary possibilities that exist beyond what may seem logical or expected.

"Expect miracles" is a phrase that has grown in popularity over the recent years, and people claim to be changing their lives attracting the life they desire. However, embracing a mindset of miracles isn't something that happens overnight. For most of us, it's a continual process that will require dedication and inspired action for the rest of our lives, but by slowly building up the tools necessary to change your perspective, you can change your life for the better.

So in this chapter, I want to discuss the areas where I have learned to embrace and build a better life for myself.

I was a real go-getter in my twenties. No matter my situation, I always found the positive in the negative. I worked in the landscaping industry for years and started my first business when I was twenty. No matter the challenge, I work toward a solution. I still remember the first large landscaping contract I won. I had been reading Richard Branson's autobiography *Losing my Virginity and* began adapting Richards's philosophy of saying yes and figuring out the how later. Even though I had never worked on a project of this magnitude, I said yes first with the goal of figuring out the "how" later. It worked! There is power in starting with a positive can-do attitude that breeds confidence and belief.

I eventually went on to build a team of 15, not including hired contractors. The initial challenge was the pressure and my lack of ability to release that pressure. I found that being responsible for managing my team and making sure the projects were completed on time was stressful. On top of this, evidently there were mistakes. For example, when one of the boys put a back roe through a water pipe, it flooded the job site in minutes. Then there is the pressure of meeting project completion dates. If they're not met then payments are delayed and it can be a strain on resources to pay wages. Looking back in reflection, having a hobby or sport would have helped. But everything happens for a reason and my meltdown led me to the root cause of the issue.

Unresolved trauma. This is a problem we know much more about today than in the late nineties. In that era, people kept their therapy sessions a secret and many considered seeking help a weakness. My mindset back then was to sweep the emotionally significant events of my childhood under the rug. There was the incident of having my face rubbed into my own feces that had fallen onto the floor as I ran to the bathroom when I was seven. The incident was never spoken of again and it had a profound impact on me. It heavily affected my mental state, especially when under pressure.

My progress of developing the miracle mindset was weighed down by an anchor of negative coping mechanisms triggered by my increased workload. Recreational drugs and partying became my way of self-medicating my emotional wounds. One by one, I lost my major contracts and quickly spiraled out of control. Things had become so bad that I moved back in with my mom and her partner. At twenty-four, it was a shameful experience that dented my confidence and self-belief. My four years as a business owner came to a dramatic end. The positive was that I eased off the recreational drugs, gaining some semblance of control over my life again.

I started reading about unresolved trauma and how that leads to adopting a negative mindset. I was surprised by what I found. It turns out that most of us are hardwired to look for the negatives in different situations, especially if we have unresolved childhood wounds. However, even though we might be hardwired to look for the negatives, how we respond to our thoughts and feelings plays a large part in how we feel in our day-to-day lives.

The articles I read and the seminars I attended mirrored my own experiences. What I read in books and learned at various personal development events confirmed that the longer I fed into a negative mindset, the harder it was to notice the positives, even if I had had an overwhelmingly positive day or experience. The past bears a heavy weight, and we need to learn to live in the present moment.

I experienced large doses of how unjust the emotional, physical, and sexual abuse was for a young child to face. Once the repressed traumas reappeared, I felt a real need to tell everyone about it, and I felt like everybody HAD TO KNOW. But the more I read about negative mindsets, the more I realized what the most essential first step in my journey to mastering my attitude had to be: healing my childhood wounds.

All sexual abuse is heinous and only serves to pass on childhood wounds from one generation to the next. After working on myself, I learned to forgive my uncle for molesting me while we were "wrestling" as other family members watched and laughed. I consider myself lucky it was an isolated incident and never happened again. But the fact that the incident was never spoken of left me feeling confused and unsure about myself.

While there were many steps in my journey to creating a mindset open to miracles, one of the biggest ones was to stop talking about the negatives. For example, I became solution-oriented when problems arose in my life. If I had an issue with something that could be fixed, I would speak up. If I was stuck in traffic, I would listen to a positive CD about mindset and manifestation or anything uplifting and educational. Instead of dreading rush-hour traffic, I learned to enjoy the experience.

Now, I want to take a moment here to say that speaking up is essential! If you are going through a hard time, are in an abusive situation, or experiencing something that you need help with, you should absolutely say something. However, I discovered in this part of my journey that complaining about something harmless is pointless; for instance, when a client doesn't pay you and you feel the need to tell the whole world about it rather than focusing on a solution or doubling down on your efforts to do an outstanding job for the majority of clients that treat you well. Sure, we might feel the need to let loose about something every now and then, but it doesn't make us feel better in the long run and can contribute to perpetuating feelings of shame and sadness. Not to mention the likelihood of repeating the momentum of negative experiences.

Furthermore, it's important to note that talking about complex subjects like grief and depression is not the same as complaining. Therefore, it is necessary to distinguish between complaining and when an issue needs to be addressed. Finally, remember not everyone around you will feel the same way, and it's important to surround yourself with friends and mentors who support and love you no matter what you're going through.

So that was step one for me. And honestly? It was effective. When I stopped talking about everything that bothered me, it gave me time to examine what needed to be said. Sometimes I would still end up speaking up about it. Still, that would only happen when I realized the thing that was bothering me seriously needed to be addressed or because it could easily be fixed. I also learned a lot more about what I wanted. I realized that I often get annoyed in loud, busy spaces, like clubs. After spending some time with that thought, I discovered I value quiet, one-on-one time with my friends, and now I enjoy my outings a lot more. I'll only visit loud spaces if it's a celebration, like a birthday or a wedding, then I can prepare myself for the experience and focus on the moment instead of the overstimulation I feel from the environment.

It's important to note that while a mindset open to miracles can be a powerful tool for personal growth and positivity, it should be balanced with a sense of realism and responsibility. Believing in miracles does not mean ignoring practicality or neglecting to take necessary actions to achieve goals.

The power of a mindset open to miracles lies in its ability to shift perceptions, instill hope, and unlock the potential for extraordinary experiences and positive transformation. One tool I used and continue to use throughout my journey toward living miracles is asking myself if my concern is paramount and if what I'm annoyed about is the thing that's bothering me.

This is an excellent tool because just taking those few extra moments to have a conversation with ourselves can help us see that the thing that's bothering us is only temporary and won't bother us thirty minutes from now. This way, when something is truly important, it will hold more weight because you'll only be bringing up the issues that truly matter instead of something that was simply a passing annoyance.

It's worth deciphering whether what's bothering you at the moment is the issue triggering you. So, for example, a lot of the problems I was having with drug addiction, I realized, were because I wasn't feeling worthy or feeling I was enough. Hence, diving deep into personal development, quitting recreational drugs altogether in 2010, and transiting out of my second landscaping company into a mindset coach and international NLP trainer helped alleviate many of the problems I had been having.

Championing miracles takes a lot of time and it is a constant process. There have been times when I have fallen back into old habits of thinking and victimhood, but now I can recognize what's happening and have the tools at hand to deal with those feelings when they pop back up.

Before I tell you another way that I expected miracles, let's revisit the tools I used to change my negative thinking into positive thinking.

1. Stop vocalizing negativity.
2. Practice gratitude.
3. Have a conversation with yourself: "Is this important? What is beyond the surface of my trigger and behavior?"

Now that I've covered how I changed my thinking from negative to positive, let's talk about how I opened my mindset to miracles to see through a lens of wonder.

At the heart of the miraculous mindset lies the lens of wonder through which one views the world. It is the conscious decision to look beyond the mundane, to see the extraordinary in the simplest of things. A miraculous mindset allows us to gaze up at the night sky and marvel at the vastness of the universe, to witness the delicate beauty of a flower, and to find poetry in the dance of falling raindrops.

Children often express their experience with a lens of wonder that is boundless finding joy the smallest of details. I embody the lens through traveling and exploring new places on earth. For the last ten years on average I would be in another country every 60 days.

I'm also location independent and over the last 12 months I have lived in Dahab, Egypt, Los Angeles, USA, Sydney, Australia, and Bali, Indonesia. The sense of awe of riding a bike down the sunset streets of LA is pure magic, or diving the red sea in Dahab with it's cornucopia of corals and fish, to embarking on ocean cliff walks with friends in the Eastern suburbs of Sydney. It doesn't matter where you are or how often you travel a sense of wonder comes from within and embracing a childlike innocence to our environment.

In essence, the Lens of Wonder serves as a bridge between the ordinary and the extraordinary. It acts as a reminder that life is a canvas painted with countless opportunities for miracles to unfold. By developing this lens, we become more open, receptive, and aligned with the possibilities that lie beyond our everyday perceptions. It ignites the fire of hope and wonder within us, making the pursuit of a miraculous mindset both transformative and enriching.

Before I close this chapter, I'll leave you with one more trick. When I find myself in a moment where I struggle with the present moment, I do something minimal. I turn on a song I like and dance until it's over. I go for a walk around the block looking for three things that are unique that I hadn't noticed before. I spend two minutes stretching or doing ten minutes of yoga. While it's not much, I know that I'll feel better in the end. Doing something small that I enjoy is much better than doing nothing. We're all human, and remember, developing a mindset open to miracles takes time.

As this chapter on the power of a mindset open to miracles comes to a close, we find ourselves at the threshold of a profound realization – that within each of us lies the extraordinary potential to shape our lives in ways that defy convention and exceed our wildest dreams. We have embarked on a journey to embrace the Lens of Wonder, to see the world through a new perspective that reveals the magic inherent in our daily existence.

In cultivating this miraculous mindset, we have learned that the key to unlocking the power of miracles lies not in denying the realities of life, but in embracing the beauty and wonder that coexists alongside them. Our journey has unveiled the strength of hope, resilience, and the creative spark that ignites when transform our negative things and a look to address our wounded inner child.

As we move forward, let us remember that the miraculous mindset is not a fleeting notion or a mere intellectual exercise. It is a lifelong practice – a conscious choice to celebrate the extraordinary in the ordinary, to find meaning in the seemingly insignificant, and to perceive the world with open-hearted curiosity.

Embracing the miraculous mindset is not a journey to a destination but a continuous unfolding of our innermost potential. It is about navigating life's twists and turns with an unwavering belief in the possibility of miracles, even in the face of adversity. As we walk this path, let us hold fast to the understanding that every setback carries the seeds of opportunity, and every challenge is an invitation to grow stronger.

In this journey, we discover that the power of a mindset open to miracles is not an external force but a reflection of the power within us. We are the architects of our realities, and our thoughts, beliefs, and actions are the brushstrokes that paint the canvas of our lives.

Let us cultivate this mindset with patience and self-compassion, for as we nurture the Lens of Wonder, it will illuminate our paths, guiding us towards the experiences that align with our deepest desires and purpose.

So, as we close this book, let us carry the torch of wonder in our hearts and let it illuminate the darkness, illuminating the way forward. Embracing the miraculous mindset, we embrace the grand tapestry of life, woven with both mystery and magic, waiting for us to unravel its boundless potential.

With each step we take, with every dream we dare to dream, may we remember the power of a mindset open to miracles, and may it serve as a beacon of hope, inspiration, and transformation, lighting the way to a life filled with wonder and awe.

"Seeing a miracle will inspire you, but knowing you are a miracle will change you."

~ Deborah Brodie

AUTHOR BIOGRAPHIES

Annette Forsythe

Annette Forsythe resides in Hackettstown, New Jersey with her husband of 41 years, Mark. They have four incredible daughters and three of the cutest grandchildren. Annette has worn many hats in her life and the role of "Nonni" tops the list. She loves music, reading, gardening and cooking for the people she loves.

Annette's college days were spent at the University of South Florida where she earned her degree in Business Administration with a minor in Psychology, she has used these skills in parenthood, her active volunteer life, and her business.

Annette is the founding partner of Netcong Physical Therapy. An expert in the field of insurance, her knowledge has helped support the success of the business over the years. NPT has served the Netcong community for over 22 years.

Annette is a Certified Growth Leader and a Certified Growth Writer for Growth-U. This is her second time collaborating with John Spender. She welcomes sharing her stories and perspective so that others may learn to see their own possibilities. In this book

she has shared many personal life stories and has tied them to her
our journey of growth. She hopes readers might see themselves
and find the courage to live their most fulfilled life. Annette
wholeheartedly believes if you do things for the right reason and
honest intentions, you will always find success.

John Spender

John Spender is a 32-time International Best-Selling co-author who didn't learn how to read and write at a basic level until he was ten. He has since traveled to more than 68 countries and territories and started many businesses leading him to create the best-selling book series A Journey Of Riches. In addition, he is an Award-Winning International Speaker and Movie Maker.

John worked as an international NLP trainer and coached thousands of people from various backgrounds through many challenges. From the borderline homeless to wealthy individuals, he has helped many people connect with their truth to create a life on their terms.

John's search for answers to living a fulfilling life has taken him to work with Native Americans in the Hills of San Diego, to the forests of Madagascar, swimming with humpback whales in Tonga, exploring the Okavango Delta of Botswana and climbing the Great Wall of China. He's traveled from Chile to Slovakia, Hungary to the Solomon Islands, the mountains of Italy, and the streets of Mexico.

Everywhere his journey has taken him, John has discovered a hunger among people to find a new way to live, with a yearning for freedom of expression. His belief that everyone has a book in them was born.

He is now a writing coach, having worked with over 400 authors from 40 countries for the A Journey of Riches series http://ajourneyofriches. com/ and his publishing house, Motion Media International, has published 32 non-fiction titles to date.

John also co-wrote and produced the movie documentary Adversity starring Jack Canfield, Rev. Micheal Bernard Beckwith, Dr. John Demartini, and many more, coming soon in 2022. And you can bet there will be a best-selling book to follow!

AFTERWORD

As we come to the end of this remarkable journey through *Being Your Own Miracle*, we hope that the words within these pages have stirred something deep within you. We have shared our stories, our triumphs, and our vulnerabilities, all with the intention of inspiring you to realize the immense power that resides within your own being.

Throughout this book, you have been invited to reflect, question, and challenge the limiting beliefs that may have held you back from recognizing your true potential. You have been encouraged to embrace the notion that miracles are not fleeting moments bestowed upon us by chance, but rather the result of our own conscious choices, actions, and beliefs. No matter the circumstances we face or the obstacles in our path, we have the capacity to rise above, to overcome, and to become the architects of our own miracles.

But let us be clear: being your own miracle does not mean that life will always be easy or devoid of challenges. It means having the courage to face adversity head-on, to seek growth in every experience, and to persist even when the road ahead seems uncertain. It means embracing the beauty of imperfection and finding strength in vulnerability.

Remember, you are not alone on this journey. Countless people have embarked on the path of self-discovery and self-empowerment before you, and many will follow. Draw strength from their collective wisdom and find solace in the shared struggles and victories of humanity. We are all interconnected, and our individual journeys contribute to the tapestry of human existence.

As you close this book, we encourage you to carry the lessons you've learned, the insights you've gained, and the inspiration you've felt into every aspect of your life. Embrace the power of intention, take consistent action towards your goals, and nourish your spirit with self-love and self-care. Trust in your own inner guidance and know that you possess the innate ability to create miracles.

Celebrate your progress, no matter how small. Every step forward is a testament to your determination and resilience. And when you stumble or face setbacks, remember that they are not signs of failure but opportunities for growth and learning. In the moments when doubt creeps in or when you find yourself wavering, come back to this book. Let the words on these pages serve as a reminder of the transformative journey you have embarked upon and the incredible potential that lies within you.

Our message is one of hope, of unwavering belief in the human spirit, and of the infinite possibilities that exist within each of us. We hope our stories have touched your heart, and it is our sincere hope that they have ignited a flame within you—a flame that will guide you towards a life filled with purpose, fulfillment, and the realization of your own miracles.

May you always remember that you are the creator of your own destiny, the architect of your own dreams, and the catalyst for the miracles that await you.

With boundless faith in your journey,

John Spender & Annette Forsythe

Also by John & Annette

In Search of Happiness: A Journey of Riches, Book Seventeen

https://www.amazon.com/dp/B07R8HMP3K

Made in the USA
Middletown, DE
16 November 2023